the **right** storage

ROCKPORT

First published in the United States of America by
Rockport Publishers, Inc.
33 Commercial Street
Gloucester, Massachusetts 01930-5089
Telephone: (978) 282-9590
Facsimile: (978) 283-2742
www.rockpub.com

ISBN 1-56496-842-1

10 9 8 7 6 5 4 3 2 1

Design: Leeann Leftwich
Production and Layout: Susan Raymond
Photo Research: Kate Holt-McLaughlin

Front Cover Images: James Salomon (right);
Courtesy of IKEA (top left);
Courtesy of Hold Everything (bottom left)
Back Cover Images: Eric Roth/Design by Phinney;
Michael Moran (bottom)

Printed in China.

the **right** storage

ORGANIZING ESSENTIALS FOR THE HOME   LISA SKOLNIK

ROCKPORT PUBLISHERS

GLOUCESTER MASSACHUSETTS

To my mother, Dorothy Zuckert, who never throws anything away, and to the sentiment she has evoked with the items she has kept all these years.

Contents

Introduction   6

Getting Storage Right   8

Storage in Living Areas   32

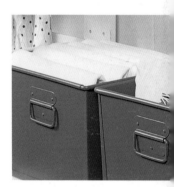

Storage in Hardworking Areas   56

All Around the House   80

Make Your Own Storage   102

Resources   **140**
Credits   **143**
Acknowledgments   **144**
About the Author   **144**

Introduction

It's virtually impossible to go through life without acquiring something to store, such as clothes, toiletries, linens, kitchen accoutrements, food, cleaning supplies, personal records, books. And most of us acquire far more than just "a bit" of any of these things. More realistic is that we have loads of clothes for every imaginable activity, scads of shoes and accessories, and masses of beauty and grooming products—not to mention weighty stacks of books, tapes, compact disks, a variety of audio-visual, electronic, and computing components, sporting goods, tools, and gardening equipment, along with substantial accumulations of collectibles.

Basically, everybody has things to store, from the avowed minimalist to the inveterate collector, which makes storage a never-ending "story" with a never-ending array of "plots." No one can afford to ignore this matter, for without the order proper and appropriate storage imposes on our effects, chaos can reign supreme. Who hasn't turned their home upside-down looking for some elusive item that wasn't to be found where it was supposed to be? Who hasn't gazed with dread at a heap of items that needs to be arranged in a manner that makes it orderly and accessible? Who hasn't spent hours cleaning, sorting, and arranging supplies, tools, or gear in various areas of our homes, only to have the order destroyed during everyday use. Getting storage right is a complex proposition that requires accurate planning and design, and vigilant execution.

Bottom line, it is critical to keep clutter from infiltrating, and ultimately overwhelming, our environments—especially since there are so many different items we need to maintain and preserve in our lives. To do this, it is essential to design storage systems that are convenient for items accessed everyday; organized for those items which are stashed away for occasional use; and safe and secure for items that will be stored long periods of time.

Remember, it's not the space, it's what you do with it—or how creatively you mine and employ the spaces at your disposal. And just as there are many approaches to home decorating and design, there are many methods for accomplishing our goals where storage is concerned as well. On the following pages, we will explore the many ways storage can be integrated into your home or teased out of unsuspecting spots you may have not considered for this use.

Getting Storage Right

For most of us, being physically disorganized is a stressful and debilitating state of being. But at the same time, the idea of getting organized fills us with anxiety, since figuring out which type of storage to use where can be a daunting and intimidating task. Further complicating matters, we usually equate neatness with organization, and the two are not one and the same. Neatly stored away doesn't necessarily mean arranged in an organized and rational manner, or making the best use of available space. It is sometimes difficult to foresee what the long-term strengths or weaknesses will be of a specific type of storage, or whether it will suit your needs. You may still not be able to easily find what you want when it's needed, or have enough room to store analogous or related items in the same place. Or you may even seriously underestimate your needs, and wind up with way too little storage space.

What's the best way to get organized and find the right place for everything we own? There is no proscribed method that will work for everyone, but there are a number of key considerations that apply to us all. There are also certain proven strategies that are helpful when it comes to taking the plunge and getting started.

opposite
Situate items near the sites where they are used in a room, and make sure to incorporate a variety of storage options. Open shelves are a sensible way to accommodate the items attractive enough to always be on view, such as hardcover books, while tapes, CDs, and videos can remain out of sight in cabinets or drawers.

right
Build enough storage space to place analogous or related items in the same area, especially when the pieces on view are part of a collection. Estimating needs correctly to create the appropriate amount of storage is a critical component in this process.

FUNDAMENTALS FIRST The types of storage to employ are as many and varied as all the items there are to store, and the best choices depend on individual wants, needs, and aesthetics. Consideration must be given to what a residence is like and the nature, make-up, lifestyle, and personal preferences of a family unit. It is also important to remember that organization and storage are virtually symbiotic, since appropriate storage leads to higher levels of organization in daily life. If you have to search frantically for something every time it's needed, or spend too much time ordering or arranging the things you own, then you aren't living in a sensibly and appropriately organized home. Of course, there does come a point when too many possessions can be counterproductive since the more we own, the more there is to care for and store. At some point, it can become necessary or advantageous to pare down and get rid of possessions instead of letting those possessions master you. But fortunately there are many storage options to explore before it is necessary to give anything away.

Different kinds of residences allow for, and incorporate, different kinds of storage. Apartments lack the roomy expanses afforded by houses that have basements, attics, crawl spaces, and utility rooms, but many newer condominiums or lofts are built with loads of empty space for this purpose, ranging from oversized closets and spacious windowless rooms to storage lockers and cages in shared common areas. And older homes often have smaller closets and bathrooms, but make up for this deficit with larger rooms that offer lots of leeway to incorporate storage. Many also possess idiosyncratic nooks and crannies, such as large foyers, extra-wide hallways, or broad stairway landings that can be utilized in alternative ways.

Family size is another obvious influence on storage needs. Children always take up more space than expected, especially when they're small and have bulky gear, such as swings, strollers, and activity toys. Older children or teens may need space for hoards of books, toys, collectibles, sporting goods, and audio-visual devices and the supplies these entail. And aging relatives may have special care needs that call for cumbersome pieces of equipment, such as walkers and wheelchairs, or caretakers who also need to be accommodated in your home. Plus, the more souls in a household, the more clothing, provisions, linens, and towels to stock in closets and cabinets in every room.

> **Look**ing For Lost Space

There are many ways to tease out more storage space in your home. Some involve making the storage spaces you are already using more efficient, while others require you to look at the spaces in new ways. The following suggestions will help you figure out which option will best suit your needs.

> **Keep Shelf Heights to a Minimum** While shelves are the most practical and efficient solution for storing a wide array of items, they can also eat up too much space when they are too widely spaced. Excess room between shelves wastes space by decreasing the storage system's capacity. This can also force you to place the items you are storing in higher piles or stacks, which can compromise the strength of the shelves and make access difficult.

> **Be Flexible** Try to only use shelves that are adjustable, and opt for more narrowly spaced shelves with lower piles of items than the other way around.

> **Mine the Space Between Shelves** If you are storing items that don't use the full space allocated by permanently fixed shelves, mine the space that is left unused. One option is to purchase wire baskets that come in varying heights and widths, slip onto shelves with wire brackets, and hang down into the empty space left above items on the shelf below. Another option is to place a wire half shelf in between two widely spaced shelves.

> **Ring Windows with Shelves** If you have a reasonable amount of space between two windows or a row of windows; between windows and walls; or underneath windows;

fill that expanse with built-in shelves. Bookshelves can be as narrow as 8 inches (20 cm) deep, yet accommodate dozens of interesting objects, while only using a small amount of floor space in a room. Consider deeper shelves underneath windows, which can also function as window seats when topped with cushions and pillows. Because shelves used to forge window seats don't go all the way up to the ceiling, they leave the visual illusion of expansiveness in a room intact.

> Don't Waste Corners Claim corner space with a triangularly shaped shelving unit, either freestanding or built in. Consider giving it doors to hide unattractive items. Kitchen corners are ideal for tucking away appliance "garages" with sliding or retractable doors that keep large unattractive appliances dust-free and out of sight. In washrooms, such corner cupboards can also accommodate a surprisingly large amount of toiletries.

> Carve Closets Out of Walls Sounds impossible, but an entire wall can become an expansive and highly efficient closet, while shaving just a few feet off the length or width of a room. Turn the space into a floor-to-ceiling wall closet and outfit it with shelves, double- or triple-hung poles, or even cubbies, depending on what you plan on using it for. Edge it with sliding doors that allow you total and efficient access to every inch inside.

> Wrest Space From Under Stairwells Storing items underneath the stairs is hardly a new idea, but it isn't often done with an eye to substance and style. Instead of just slapping a door on the space and making it a closet, consider a variety of other options. Fit the space with built-in shelves, a built-in storage chest with pullout drawers, or even an entire home office. Or, build a bench from one end to the other with storage for boots, hats, and gloves underneath, and cushions for seating on top.

below
Tease still more storage out of a space by ringing windows with built-in cabinets and/or shelves.

MORE KEY CONSIDERATIONS Your lifestyle and personal preferences, which dictate how you spend your time and what you find appealing or unattractive, may seem unrelated to storage, but these considerations actually have a major impact on how you use your home and what you put in it.

If you have a large family or an active social life and frequently cook or entertain, you may need lots of storage in your kitchen for pots and pans, dishware, and table linens, or an area in your home to manage the piles of papers related to the activities and engagements of every-day life. If you work at home, you'll need space for the collateral materials, such as computer equipment, files, and supplies. Or if you have a hobby, such as a particular sport, gardening, woodworking, reading, painting, sewing, knitting, or even surfing the Internet, you will also need room to store all the related accouterments. And if the gear these call for isn't organized and easy to access, it can be difficult and inconvenient to enjoy these activities.

Personal proclivities are also surprisingly important. Some favor storage that incorporates display, while others want to hide everything away to create a sleek and ordered environment. But the issue is not quite this cut and dry, since a system that incorporates storage and display at the same time affords many advantages. It not only offers easy access to frequently used items, it can, if properly executed, make accumulations of objects look handsome or striking.

Also, the potential display value of everyday objects is often over-

looked, and employing systems that combine storage and display

can be the most sensible and efficient solution in many cases. On

the other hand, this method can be overdone, with way too much

left in the open to appear cluttered and collect dust. Concealed

storage also has its strengths and weaknesses. It can be elegant

and sleek, and everything is in its own spot. But it often necessi-

tates installing costly built-ins, and putting everything back right

where it belongs requires discipline. There's always the option of a

happy medium, where prized or interesting possessions are put on

show and mundane items are stowed away. But even achieving this

balance isn't easy.

GETTING STARTED So how can you plan adequate and appropriate storage for your home? Obvious as it sounds, begin with the basics and keep your family size, lifestyle, aesthetics, and budget in mind. Organizing a home doesn't always call for major upheavals or exorbitant expense, but it does call for employing a consistent, ordered, and logical approach that takes every area of your home into consideration on a case by case basis.

Start with macro-planning—assess and address your overall storage needs. Go from room to room in your home with notepad in hand and visualize what goes on in the room for an entire day. Think about who uses the room, what they usually do in it, what stays out, and what gets put away. Then consider whether there is already enough storage space in these rooms, or whether you need to devise more. If you answer the latter, consider whether storage can be created through the use of furnishings and/or built-in systems, or if you need to find additional storage areas in other parts of your home, such as the attic, basement, or garage.

Micro-planning is the next step to making the most of storage in a home. The areas in each room that house—or will house—clusters of stuff, such as cabinets, closets, and shelves, must be installed, organized, and constantly pruned to keep belongings in check and prevent you from outgrowing what storage space you do have.

Ultimately, while some do design and install new systems for storage, or even add on more space, many are forced to, or prefer to, work with the systems or storage spaces that are already there. Cabinets can be refurbished, shelves can be reconfigured, closets can be refitted, and dead spaces can be transformed into islands of storage with the right tools.

above
Using open shelving, such as this industrial system for pots and pans, is a great way to maintain order in a space. The nature of the system forces you to stay organized and keep everything in check to keep the room presentable and prevent your possessions from outgrowing the allotted storage space.

opposite
Organizing your home calls for using the systems that are already in place to maximum advantage. Built-in storage that incorporates open and closed recesses allows you to put attractive items on display and functional ones away. Best of all, adjustable shelves can be reconfigured to accommodate a variety of items, while the area behind closed doors can be filled to capacity without disturbing the aesthetics in a room.

> **Macro**-Planning

> **Take Stock of Everything You Own** Experts advise you to go through every area of your home, and evaluate, categorize and purge. Chances are, you can easily pare down, especially since there is no reason to save what you don't like, need, or use. These items only take up space and promote clutter. After going through this process, you should be left with what really counts: the things you want to save for sentimental purposes, what you use everyday, seasonal items, and what you need sporadically.

> **Assess What's Left** Separate items into categories based on how frequently you use them. Items on demand every day need to be readily accessible. Things used on a seasonal basis or only sometimes still need to be relatively accessible. Items that are rarely used, or that you are saving for future use, can be

put away. Be sure to keep a list of what gets stowed away in long-term storage to make retrieval easier and help you remember what you have.

> **Take Stock of How You Use Your Rooms** This will give you an idea of all the space you have at your disposal. Re-allocating these spaces sometimes makes sense. For instance, a formal dining room can be combined with, or even turned into, a library for someone with a massive book collection. Or, a master suite can be used to accommodate a home gym or become a bedroom and a play area for a few children, freeing up several smaller rooms to be assigned new uses.

> **Take Stock of Auxiliary Spaces** Most homes have spaces that aren't part of specific rooms—the areas under stairs,

extra-large landings, or spacious circulation corridors—but offer up lots of square footage to adapt to storage. Just be careful that you don't impinge on traffic patterns in your home.

> **Decide on an Overall Approach for Each Space** Ask yourself what kind of storage will work best in each area. Can freestanding furnishings yield the appropriate amount and type of storage you need, or would built-ins be more efficient and economical? Should storage be open to expose its contents, or enclosed to hide everything behind closed doors? Will creative structural solutions be necessary, such as giving a crowded kitchen a "space"-lift by carving out a pantry or concealing an entire home office behind a false wall?

_**opposite**
A wraparound set of shelves paired with a comfortable reading chair and adequate lighting turns a corner of a room into a library and incorporates attractive display spaces.

above
Fine-tune the large spaces on
shelves and in cabinets with bins
that can keep smaller or oddly
shaped items neatly in place.

MAKING CHOICES To plan storage intelligently, it's important to know all your options. And these days, options abound thanks to the proliferation of home design stores and mass merchandisers stocking storage products. There are literally thousands of items to choose from, ranging from boxes, baskets, carts, and bins to shelving systems of every ilk. And these products are made from myriad materials and executed in every decorative style, which is advantageous for some but problematic for the indecisive. Also, knowing your storage needs doesn't mean you know what products will best fulfill these needs, and with so many options to choose from, the process can get confusing.

Take the time to acquaint yourself with all the options and get a comprehensive overview of what's available to use "as is" and what you might adapt to your needs. Mail-order catalogs, mass merchandisers, discounters, and housewares chains—including specialty bed and bath stores—offer a huge range of storage products that will work for every room in the home, while home design centers and/or department stores sell decorative, singular, or even exotic pieces that are also storage alternatives. Collect catalogs to peruse, comparing the costs, sizes, materials, and flexibility of the options available.

Start out with easy-to-use, economical options before committing to pricey storage systems and/or built-ins. For instance, fit out a closet, home office, bathroom, or kid's room with inexpensive, store-bought components and live with them a while to see what best fits your needs and addresses your space demands. You can always opt for costly structural changes or built-ins later when you are more definite about what will work for you.

right
Create your own custom system
with components that allow you to
build shelving to your own specifi-
cations. One advantage of these
systems is they can be reconfigured in many different dimensions
to meet your changing needs.

> **Micro-**Planning

> **Work on One Room at a Time** Instead of being intimidated by the huge project of reorganizing your entire home, take the room that needs the most shaping up, or is most critical to you on a daily basis, and start there. Ascertain what needs to be stored in that room, determine what kind of storage systems will fulfill your goals in the most efficient and economical way, and execute the easiest ones first. For instance, if you can't afford the beautiful built-in shelves you want, start with a temporary freestanding alternative that can later be re-used elsewhere in your home.

> **Group Like Items** Function is the most obvious common denominator. It is logical and easy to have items with the same purpose or use in one central, easily accessible spot. Or break whole categories down into smaller groups. Divide a wardrobe by shirts, skirts, pants, ties, and shoes, or an assortment of tableware by platters, vases, crystal, dishes, and so on.

> **Keep Convenience in Mind** Some things are obvious: CDs, tapes, and remote controls should be stored close to audio-visual equipment and everyday dishes should be right near the kitchen table. But don't forget about the other items you need or use on a daily basis. For instance, if you like to knit or do your nails while watching television, or play games in your kitchen or study, store these items close to where they'll actually be used.

> **Be Open to Revamping Storage Solutions** Sometimes it takes time to work out the best system to meet your requirements, since identifying your storage goals and figuring out how to fulfill them may not be readily apparent. It can take some trial and error, especially when an entire family is involved, because everyone's wants and needs change. Storage solutions must evolve; don't hesitate to make changes when they're necessary.

> **Rotate and Review Long-term Storage Twice a Year** Keep a survey of everything you have in long-term storage. Force yourself to change your seasonal items on a timely basis so you get use out of them, and reevaluate the things you plan on keeping in storage to make sure you aren't holding on to things that have become totally useless.

above
This novel approach follows some basic tenets of good micro-planning. Like items, namely a whole set of colorful fiberglass chairs, are grouped together, and one tiny corner has been turned into an attractive and creative storage space.

left
Stow the items used in a specific area close at hand for convenience. A set of baskets stashed underneath a sofa can hold papers, books, or the remote control and vastly improve the efficiency of the setting.

below
The basics here, namely a display ledge and a set of side tables, create a stunning foundation that also offers the right kind and amount of storage for this glamorous bedroom.

BLENDING FUNCTION AND FORM Storage doesn't have to be unattractive, unimaginative, or prosaic. Accessories such as decorative boxes, baskets, and bowls, some of which are art objects in their own right, and case goods, ranging from antique to contemporary cabinets, armoires, chests, sideboards, and trunks, are as important for their storage function as well as for their alluring or interesting forms. Look at these items as a means to two ends, since they can be used to decorate your home and keep it clutter-free at the same time. Also keep in mind that you may already have many of these items on hand, making it unnecessary to go out and acquire them.

Evaluate the items you already own. Since your accessories or furnishings were acquired for their aesthetic value and are already integrated into your decorating scheme, you might as well make the most of them. Don't let a set of hand-woven baskets or Shaker boxes sit empty, or under-utilize an antique cabinet or chest.

Baskets, boxes, and bowls make attractive and practical containers for a surprisingly wide range of items, including jewelry, makeup, craft tools, office supplies, hair accessories, and more. Matching or coordinating sets of these accessories can even be used to fine-tune masses of like items. For efficiency categorize bracelets, necklaces, earrings, and watches, or threads, buttons, and sewing notions into several containers instead piling everything into one.

All aesthetically pleasing furnishings are not created equal when it comes to storage capacity. A leggy sideboard with a few narrow drawers won't be as capacious as a more massive piece with drawers from head to foot, yet it will occupy the same volume and floor space. A stately, high-set bed can have shelves built-in underneath the mattress if the room is short of floor space for dressers or chests. A bench in a foyer can have an enclosed bottom to hide boots, hats, scarves, and gloves. Keep storage considerations in mind when choosing furnishings for your rooms.

opposite
Make the most of the accessories or furnishings you already own for their aesthetic value. A collection of primitive chests and Depression-era tins offer up plenty of empty space that can be put to good use storing all sorts of items in a kitchen.

above
There are many creative ways to eliminate clutter. A skirted table provides a surface to showcase objects and art, and provides conveniently situated hidden storage.

opposite
Always keep convenience in mind. Shelves stationed right above a sofa allow books to be stored out of the way, but easily accessed when wanted.

> **Getting Organized** for Good Feng Shui

Feng shui is the ancient Chinese practice of placing or arranging furniture and objects in a space. While architecture and interior design are concerned with structure, form, function, and visual aesthetics, feng shui takes into account the conscious and unconscious associations we have with a space, the things that are in it, and the placement of everything within that space. Good feng shui is said to improve the flow of energy in a space and bring about increased prosperity, health, and personal success.

The first step to achieving good feng shui is to clear away clutter, to cleanse the space and ultimately create a home that nurtures and embraces. Since your home is supposed to mirror your inner self, you will feel physically and emotionally liberated once you have done this. It will also eliminate the obstructions that prevent good energy from flowing through your rooms and bring about positive changes in your life.

Of course, too many possessions can be counter-productive, since the more we own, the more there is to care for and store. Paring down allows you to let go of possessions before they take hold of you. But no matter how rational and realistic you are, throwing anything away is often hard to do. Yet it's a necessary evil if you hope to get uncluttered and keep your possessions in check.

> **Set Reasonable Goals**
You can't—and won't—get rid of everything all at once. Don't even expect to un-clutter an entire room in one day. Instead, pick the area that troubles you most, establish a time limit, and get to work. Make sure you finish one area before moving on to the next.

> **Plan Your Attack**
Examine each item and decide to do one of three things: keep it, give it away, or put it in long-term storage. To decide what you should toss or save, take a cue from fashion advisors who tell you to unload garments you haven't worn in over a year. If you haven't used something and still feel it's worth keeping, relegate it to long-term storage.

> **Categorize** Form three piles: one for active storage that is easily accessible; one for long-term, inactive storage; and one for items you plan on unloading. Immediately bag up the items you're tossing and put them where they won't be in the way, like the trunk of your car.

> **Box or Bag up Items for Inactive Storage** Do this before you put stuff you will be actively using away. Use a clear plastic box or bag; otherwise be prepared to label it. Make a list of what's in each container and where it's going, and stash it away in relatively inaccessible spots, such as high shelves, crawl spaces, or out-of-the-way closets.

> **Deal With the Everyday Stuff** Put things you use frequently in accessible spaces: in drawers and on shelves within your reach, on countertops, in centrally located closets, and so on. You may not come up with the best setup for putting these items away immediately, but you will have made a good start towards placing them where they need to be and can always fine-tune your system later.

> **Organizing** Your Stuff

Clever storage solutions and ideas
for the way you really live

right
A steel cart can be put to work in any room to hold a variety of items, be it food, clothes, papers, or audio-visual supplies. The industrial look of steel is great with art deco or modernist furnishings.

right
Keep magazine and newspapers ordered and attractive with a divided wicker basket. Bring decorative details into play when possible—matching the basket material to the colors and motifs of the room.

right
Economical modular shelving systems can be pieced together anywhere in your home to emulate built-ins. Use them in the hardest working areas—such as kitchen, garage, and laundry areas—and as excellent storage solutions for tight spaces under eaves or stairs.

right

Pullout CD storage makes it easier to access the disk that you desire. For placement—make sure to balance the shape of storage against the objects nearby, so that the visual "weight" of each is complementary.

right

Hanging stainless steel bins can organize all your paperwork. Hanging storage is often overlooked, and is a wonderful way to make the most of small spaces.

right

Baskets can be used alone or stacked on shelves. Baskets in groups of three are especially successful and easy on the eye. Groups of an odd number of objects make better displays than even-number displays.

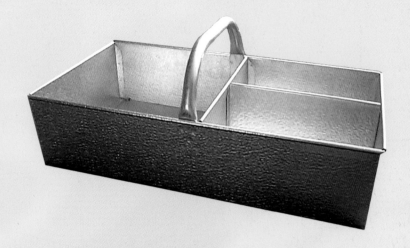

right
A steel basket may seem like the perfect desk accessory, but be creative. It can also hold jewelry, makeup, and more. Steel accessories look contemporary and sleek and are a nice mix when paired with more traditional wooden furnishings.

right
A steel magazine rack adds structure and style to stacks of periodicals: Strong and serviceable—but still stylish.

right
An industrial tool tray with a fascinating shape can provide storage for the small things in life and add panache to a space. Open storage works best when you pare down the items to those most-used.

Storage in Living Areas

How much do you really use your living room? Is it basically reserved for relaxing and entertaining, or do you use it for a much broader range of activities? And what about your dining room or bedroom? Are they used only for the functions they were designed to accommodate, namely eating and sleeping, or do you also sneak in a few tasks, such as working on projects at the dining room table or exercising in your bedroom?

Regardless of how you use the living spaces in your home, flexible storage solutions are key to organizing them to be multifunctional and efficient. In fact, most of the living spaces in our homes are open to new interpretations as our lifestyles evolve and change. And most of the rooms in our homes are used in more ways than ever before, which greatly influences the way they are furnished and the kind of storage now included in their bounds.

Carving out good-looking storage for all the trappings of contemporary life can be challenging. While all storage units are similar in substance—as they all hold things—they can be quite different in style. Built-ins can be fashioned in any decorative form—be it colonial, Arts and Crafts, ethnic, or high-tech—and freestanding units come in shapes that range from frothy vintage armoires to sleek post-Modern cabinets.

Manipulating storage is another issue, since both built-ins and freestanding pieces can either fade into the background or be used to define a room. Natural recesses (such as alcoves or the spaces surrounding mantels) or whole blank walls are ideal and unobtrusive spots for both built-in or freestanding storage (especially if the freestanding piece fits the niche exactly and mimics a built-in). But large shelving systems, or even shorter units placed back-to-back, can also become room dividers.

opposite
Storage can help define the way your living space functions. Here, a whole wall of built-in shelving houses a large library yet allows the living area to be unencumbered. It can be used for reading or entertaining guests.

> **Decorating** With Storage

Storage is more than a practical element that can organize your environment. Depending on the type you choose, it can also be used to divide an open-plan space, such as a loft or a large room that serves several functions, into zones. Or, it can add a considerable amount of decorative cache to a space.

How can you achieve both ends with storage? Opt for pieces or systems that blend function and form. Make sure these pieces have a definite perspective from a decorative standpoint. For instance, a shelving unit in the vein of a specific ethnic or period style can be used to carve a room or space into distinct zones, and at the same time lend a whole room its demeanor.

There is also an infinite range of smaller pieces to consider, which can be used in conjunction with shelves and case goods, or alone. While they won't have the same space-defining potential as large storage pieces, they can fine-tune a space and complement larger storage pieces. For instance, pretty wicker baskets or sleek metal bins can be stacked all alone, or fit into a shelving system to hold and hide smaller items. Boxes, chests, crates, and containers are also options, and can all be used in interesting or downright creative ways to further a specific attitude or style in a room, while providing storage.

> **Period Style** Formality, symmetry, and detailing are the benchmarks of most period pieces. Built-in and freestanding storage units should be graced with hardware, molding, and finishes (using paint or stains) that imbue them with a specific demeanor, be it Baroque, neo-Classical, Regency, Federal, or Victorian.

> **Country Style** Country style is extremely broad and culturally diverse, and can be expressed in a number of different ways. Pieces can be rustic and quaint, primitive and austere, or even stately and refined. But in general, country pieces are fabricated from wood or veneers designed to mimic wood, and display a distinct simplicity of form and design.

> **Ethnic Style** Many ancient cultures developed storage options that were designed to be portable, such as stacking and nesting baskets from all over Asia, wooden merchant's chests from Europe, and woven saddlebags and sacks from the Middle East. These items are straightforward, simple, and striking, and work well in contemporary interiors as storage solutions.

> **Modern Style** Modern furniture has its roots in the Arts and Crafts and Prairie movements. Pieces used to evoke this style can range from the rich, dark wooden pieces that were crafted by artisans at the beginning of the twentieth century to the sleek metal machine age pieces developed during the Art Deco and Modernist eras. To most, Modern style is still exemplified by the stylized yet streamlined pieces that were so popular in the fifties.

> **Contemporary Style** The plastic storage cube revolutionized storage options in the seventies, and started a trend towards modular storage pieces that can be used stacked or set next to each other to forge large, flexible systems. Today, standard residential furniture lines as well as industrial and contract pieces are all employed by homeowners to create storage systems in homes.

above
Bamboo shelving units, coupled with a split-reed wall treatment and woven chairs imbue this space with an airy, Asian aesthetic. The shelves also provide plenty of storage for books and define the room's layout by creating two distinct and intimate spaces.

LIVING ROOMS Living rooms are rarely the stiff showpieces they once were, for few of us have space to waste. We truly live in this room these days, and use it for both formal and informal activities. Family members are just as likely to plop down in here after a hard day to relax, read, listen to music, or watch television, as they are to entertain guests in the space. Considering these functions, the living room must be comfortable and nurturing as well as presentable and attractive.

Today's living room must incorporate a wide range of items. There may be large pieces of audio-visual equipment to hide away along with all the accompanying accessories, like a huge stock of CDS, tapes, and videos as well as reading materials. Not to mention the objects we want to have on show, such as prized possessions, artworks, and collectibles, necessitating open storage for display.

Storage in living rooms is key to a clutter-free, smoothly functioning environment, and the challenge is to find options that are utilitarian, versatile, and subtle enough not to disrupt the integrity of the interior design of the space. For instance, the books or CDs that are stored here must not only be orderly and accessible, they must be housed in systems or pieces that are handsome and blend with the décor of the room.

Fortunately, there are many ways to accomplish this. Construct permanent cabinets or shelves flanking both sides of a fireplace and use decorative moldings to give these storage centers a more formal and decorative demeanor. Or, build a banquette skirting a bay or picture window, with lift-up or sliding doors that allow access to the storage space they create and elegant cushions to enhance their comfort and appearance.

opposite
Keep a living room clutter-free with cleverly concealed storage options. An antique chest that does double duty as a coffee table keeps miscellaneous items out of sight in this space.

DINING AREAS As with living rooms, dining rooms can be combined with libraries, entertainment areas, home offices, family rooms, and even kitchens—which is quite a feat if a semblance of formal decorum is important to the homeowner. And they often serve as a space for displaying collectibles, especially if these objects are related to dining. So there may be all sorts of other items to incorporate into the dining room scheme along with the usual trappings, like china, silver, linens, and serving pieces.

The traditional dining room fare, such as breakfronts, buffets, cupboards, and dressers, are good places to start when looking for ways to keep clutter from overwhelming the space. These pieces offer up plenty of storage space as well as adequate surface area to serve food and beverages during meals. Plus, many of these pieces can be modified or customized to accommodate special needs, such as oversized serving pieces and fragile stemware—or even an entire home office if necessary.

To eke more space out of a dining area, built-ins are the most viable option. Build shelves along walls or into corners, and front these with doors to create cabinets and cupboards. Line windows and walls with custom banquettes that feature storage underneath, or slip elegant chests and baskets under benches that can also be pulled up to a table to provide extra seating. And even a simple plate rail can be multiplied to become an installation on a wall that can hold an entire set of china.

_**above**
Built-ins do double duty in this dining room by providing plenty of storage and serving space.

_**opposite**
A sideboard can be all that is needed to make a dining space more functional, since it can hold dining accoutrements and provide a place to serve meals.

> **Types** of Storage

To stay organized, selecting the right kind of storage system is as important as maintaining it. The most efficient alternatives will maximize the space and options that you have in any given area. It may be necessary to combine several types of storage in a room, and the choices are seemingly endless, ranging from open or closed systems that are freestanding or built in, with fittings that are fixed or adjustable, and stationary or pullout. Plus, specific systems or units can be planned to embrace a wide variety of options at the same time.

> **Adjustable** The surfaces in an adjustable system can be easily rearranged or reconfigured, and it should be possible to do this without any tools. This type of system is useful anywhere, but particularly in closets as hem lengths go up and down and the proportion of skirts or pants we own varies. Look for systems that employ high-quality fittings so it is easy to adjust these systems alone. You may also want the hardware concealed if the storage unit is open.

> **Built-in** By nature, these systems must be custom built, are permanent, and can be more expensive than other options. But built-ins also make the most efficient use of available space, can be used in oddly sized spaces that are hard to mine with commercial options, and are sturdier

than their freestanding counterparts. They can also be used to add panache to a room.

> **Closed** Anything stashed in these systems is concealed behind closed doors or in drawers. While closed storage presents a neat appearance and protects items from dust, view, and tampering, it does limit retrieveability and the ability to display collectibles.

> **Fixed** Nothing moves in these systems; what you see stays where it is. These units offer limited flexibility and can't be adjusted to meet changing needs, but are sturdier and stronger than adjustable shelves so they can be used for heavier items. They also lack hardware that can detract from their appearance.

> **Freestanding** Anything that stands on its own, from a shelving unit or chest of drawers to cabinets and chests, is technically freestanding storage. While you are locked into a particular size and shape with these pieces, and they are, for the most part, not adjustable, they can be moved anywhere as needs change. Some of these pieces can even be put on wheels to increase their flexibility.

> **Modular** A typical modular system is a shelving system that includes bookshelves, display shelves, drawers, a pullout surface, and more. These units are comprised of components that can work all on their own or together, and must be assembled to fit a certain space. The pieces vary in length, width, and depth to create a variety of options. These systems can also be broken down and reused elsewhere.

> **Open** Everything shows in an open system, which means that neatness counts. These are ideal for display and accessibility, but require more maintenance to keep them orderly and dust-free. They can also be combined with closed storage.

> **Pullout** Though drawers are the first thing to come to mind when this term is mentioned, this type of system is also used for shelves—even whole stacks of shelves. They improve visibility and accessibility, especially in deep spaces, but can be costly.

> **Stationary** Stationary systems sport shelves that can be repositioned within the unit. But they do not slide out; they stay put. They offer more side-to-side space since they don't require the hardware that pullouts do, but can make cleaning or retrieving items more difficult.

above
Use a freestanding storage cabinet to make a statement that blends style and substance. This attractive armoire emphasizes a specific decorative aesthetic, and keeps the necessities of life out of sight.

MULTIPURPOSE FAMILY ROOMS AND GREAT ROOMS

A multipurpose space is generally used by each family member for different purposes. Some family members may like to read the paper, play games, or watch television here, while others may use it for projects, crafts, and homework. Storage must be carefully thought out because of the different functions that occur in this space, which can require a great deal of stashing and organizing of items essential to several different tasks.

While there are a number of ways to create storage in this type of space, the most important point to keep in mind is accessibility. If the storage spot for something is difficult to access or poorly organized, it is unlikely that things will get put away. For instance, if a cabinet for videos is so chockfull it can't accommodate any more tapes, or the shelf that holds games is too high for kids to reach, these storage options are destined to be failures. Both adults and kids will find a way to get what they want, but putting it away is a different matter. Storage in these spaces must be a one-step process.

What are the options? Front an entire wall with a system of shelves hidden behind sliding doors. The doors can be treated in a decorative manner that creates visual interest in the room, and keeps disorderly shelves out of sight. Shelves can also be outfitted with organizers to meet specific needs, and because they are hidden by doors, they don't necessarily have to be pretty. Another option is to build a two-part system against a wall, putting enclosed storage on the bottom and open cubbies at waist level or higher for items that need to be accessible. If still more storage is needed, cabinets can be built as high as the ceiling, but keep in mind that these shelves will be best for items not needed everyday.

opposite
Incorporate several different types of storage in a multipurpose great room to define different activity areas. Gently curved built-in cabinetry flanking a wall by the room's entry provides storage for a family's possessions, while cabinetry along the length of the area turns one wall into an entire home office.

above
Remember that storage must be accessible or it ends up being ignored. Items won't be used or properly put away. A rolling ladder makes these extra-high cubbies easy to reach.

opposite
When a bed is placed against a wall, it is possible to surround it with a system of cabinets that provides all the storage and display space that is necessary in the room.

above left
Built-in shelves offer up storage that is on show, while oversized ottomans with lift-off lids provide cleverly concealed storage spaces.

above right
The way a bed is situated in a room dictates the storage scenarios that are possible. When a bed is set smack in the middle of the bedroom, consider converting an entire wall into a closet to provide adequate storage space.

BEDROOMS   With space at a premium, bedrooms are also becoming more multi-purpose. While they are still devoted to sleeping and dressing, they can also incorporate furnishings, equipment, and accessories devoted to many other pursuits, such as shelves filled with books, a cushy chair for reading, a home office, or gym gear.

The one thing all bedrooms obviously have in common is the bed, which can, and often does, dominate the space. The way this furnishing is situated in the room dictates storage scenarios. For instance, placing a bed in the middle of a wall can create alcoves, while moving it towards one corner leaves room for larger storage units. Placing it in the middle of a space grants lots of creative leeway: the area between the bed and wall can become a dressing room, private study, or home office bounded by a shelving system, while its back can become a headboard for the bed. In virtually every situation, the area under the bed can become another source of storage, and free-standing or built-in pieces can be integrated into all these potential layouts.

But when planning a bedroom, you must not forget that it is still primarily a sleeping space, and as such, must nurture and soothe its occupants. This means that distractions must be kept to a minimum and the space relatively clutter-free. Items used for other activities, such as work or exercise gear that occupies a corner of the room, should be kept out of sight. Camouflage these in some form of storage that hides them completely, or even front them with a sedate screen if no other options are available.

> **Good Feng Shui** in Living Areas

If a room is packed with furniture and cluttered with too much stuff, the flow of energy, which is also called chi in feng shui, will stagnate. This, in turn, will create an uneasy and disturbing atmosphere that will be counter-productive since it will deter family members and guests from using the room. However, some basic principles of feng shui can be used to improve the energy flow in the space.

Feng shui dictates that the major pieces of furniture in a room should be positioned so that whoever uses them will face the room's entrance. However, this principle cannot be rigidly enforced since there are other factors that also play a big role in determining good feng shui. You have to consider the whole picture in each room, and determine whether certain floor plans and configurations of furnishings and accessories are powerful, balanced, or weak given the context of the space and what it holds.

In living spaces, clutter will deter family members and guests from lingering. Pare down wherever possible and keep things in order. Books should be on shelves, displays of framed photos contained to specific areas, magazines and newspapers stashed in a designated container, audio-visual materials organized for easy access, and knickknacks minimized. Furniture should be clutter-free and positioned around an anchor, such as a coffee table or hearth, so pieces can face each other and make it easy for people to interact.

opposite
Plenty of storage to keep the bedroom clutter-free is critical to letting you enjoy a serene environment. But storage and a bed on wheels provides even more flexibility, since it allows you to change the angle of the bed so everything else in the space is out of sight and mind when it's time to get some sleep.

In the bedroom, make sure there is plenty of storage to hold all your possessions. Things should be out of sight and furnishings should be streamlined in this space to create the soothing, peaceful atmosphere necessary to promote the primary function of this space—namely getting a good night's sleep. That means audio-visual equipment and home offices should be stored in cabinets that can be closed, work-out equipment stashed away in a closet or behind a screen, and surfaces kept relatively unencumbered.

In all your rooms, surround yourself with items you love and really use, since these will produce the sort of positive energy that will make the atmosphere optimistic and joyful. They will also provide the kind of emotional sustenance that is nurturing and supportive. Unwanted or useless items will only pull you down and make you feel encumbered.

STORAGE IN KIDS' ROOMS Children are notorious for amassing toys of every size, making major messes, and not putting things away. After only a short while, their room or play area can look like a cyclone hit. It's also the rare child who puts his clothes away rather than tossing them on the floor. And this situation doesn't change when they are teens, although their spatial needs do.

A chaotic sea of stuff and inappropriate storage options can disrupt children's lives at every stage of development. Toddlers can become frustrated with the jumble, especially if they can't find what they want. They are also not capable of negotiating some types of storage, such as shelves or bins situated too high or systems that are too complex for them to keep in order. Disarray will also thwart older children, especially when it's school books or soccer uniforms they're searching out. They also need clutter-free spaces for doing homework and for pursuing projects.

So what storage options meet a child's changing and growing needs? Storage in children's rooms must adapt and grow as they do to accommodate new and changing functions. Plan to use several types of storage in the space, since it will be necessary to accommodate a wide range of items, such as toys (which run from big and bulky to tiny and fragile), books, audio-visual equipment, clothes, and school supplies. Containers that can be used in different configurations and adjustable shelves are ideal to start with, since these will be viable for a long time, if not forever. You can also expand these systems easily by adding to them. Remember that small children need storage that is low enough for them to reach and childproof so they don't try to climb on it. Older children and teens are more likely to clean up if they have stylish and easy-to-use storage.

_right
Open shelving is ideal for young children since it can be arrayed in many ways. Here, toys and blankets are stashed well within children's reach, while books are stored on the higher shelves.

above
Think creatively about storage. An object that was never meant to be used for storage can take on a whole new dimension and be put to good use, such as this wire dress form transformed into a rack for coffee mugs.

below
A vintage metal china cabinet is perfect for storing and showing off your dishwares.

> **Tapping** Into Exotic Options

Since storage can take virtually any incarnation, it offers the perfect opportunity to creatively blend function and form. Why opt for a prosaic cabinet or chest of drawers when there are so many novel alternatives that can add a powerful presence to a room. Singular pieces of art furniture, ethnic artifacts, industrial furnishings, architectural salvage, and interesting possessions that seem like unlikely candidates can actually be mined for their storage potential. Given that these are remarkable pieces in their own right, they can also take center stage in a room or merely add a touch of interest or whimsy the environment.

> **Artist and Ethnic Pieces** For storage that becomes the center of attention, a one-of-a-kind artist-made cabinet or chest can make the most impact. Or, for something equally stunning but a bit more subdued, look into ethnic pieces from all over the world. Some are totally utilitarian, such as kitchen *tansus* from China or blanket boxes from Korea, and offer up large-scale storage space. Others are smaller, or even diminutive, as they were originally intended for portable storage, such as camel saddlebags from the Middle East, stacking and nesting baskets from Japan, lunchboxes from Burma, wedding baskets from China, and wooden spice merchant's chests from India. But all can be put to use as sources of storage for the sundry items of life.

> **New Uses for Old Pieces** Other potential storage pieces take on a different demeanor with a change of venue. Industrial furnishings that were meant for the factory or office, such as steel and metal medical supply cases, metal lockers and storage cubes, shelving with wire baskets, and even file cabinets, can be stripped, repainted, or even left

bare and used to provide useful yet arresting storage. Consider being inventive with these pieces. For example, stack a variety of old file cabinets in different colors against the same wall, *tansu* style, to create a stepped storage unit. Architectural salvage, such as cabinets, shelves, or even lengths of old wood, can also be recycled and reused in a new environment. Consider turning the vintage cases used to hold stock in stores into dressers in a bedroom, or threading planks of old wood through a ladder for a rustic shelving unit.

> **Other Alternatives** Perhaps the most fascinating storage options are the ones that were never intended for storage, and which take on a whole new dimension when used for this purpose. For instance, attractive vintage suitcases can be stacked and crowned with a glass top to become a table; printer's drawers can be finished off with a Plexiglas sheet and used to stash jewelry; and sculptural objects such as old glove molds, statues, dress forms, and hat forms can be used to hold a variety of wardrobe accessories.

right
Mine the profusion of ethnic pieces from all over the world to use as exotic storage in your own home. Many of these pieces were made as portable storage for nomadic cultures.

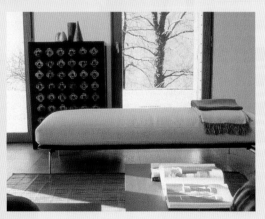

> **Organizing** Your Stuff

Clever storage solutions and ideas
for the way you really live.

below
Translucent glass doors take a bit of
pressure off the need to keep items on
shelves totally ordered. Closed storage is a good match for items that are
awkward to keep organized—such as
remote-control units, earphones, children's toys, and more.

above
A boldly colored cabinet on wheels
can make the rounds: use it to up
the style quotient of any room in
the home. There is no reason why
storage has to fade into the background—colorful storage can
anchor or accent a whole room.

When extra storage is needed in
a dining area, opt for a cabinet
system with glass doors on top to
show off dishes and serving pieces.

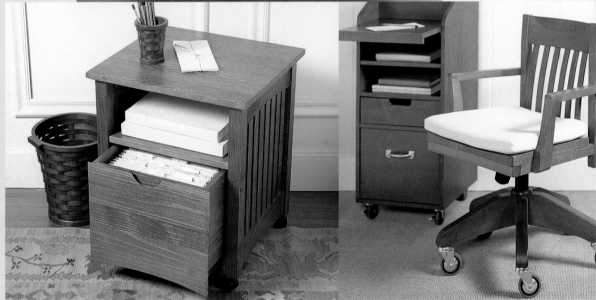

top
CD storage can take a variety of decorative forms, such as this Mission style box. Flexible, portable storage solutions are ideal for CDs, since the location of stereo equipment is changeable.

above left
An attractive file trolley with Mission styling also has a work surface to increase its utility. Trolleys are a nearly ideal storage solution: accessible and moveable, they can be brought to work areas and easily stowed out of sight when not in use.

above right
Make use of every inch of space by turning any corner of the house into a spot for writing letters or paying bills with this compact mini-office on wheels. When purchasing units such as this one, make sure the top is a material sturdy enough to support the weight of your work supplies.

right

Inexpensive tower storage is a great space-saver—stack towers with the most used objects (here they are CDs) at eye level and above, and the items you use less frequently lower to the floor. The rotating tower shown here uses a minimal amount of floor space to store a large number of CDS.

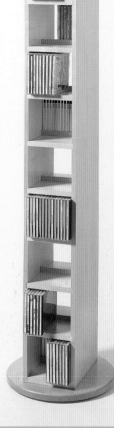

above

Collapsible shelving units that can also be stacked are ideal when temporary or moveable storage is called for. These units work especially well in children's rooms or offices, places where storage may need to be reconfigured to suit changing uses.

right

Shelves capped with drawers provide a more formal demeanor in a room. For tidier looking under-counter storage, stack in boxes of the same color and material. Fill them with equipment or tools that you need to keep, but just can't find a good space for anywhere else.

Storage in Hardworking Areas

Some rooms have a greater demand for storage spaces than others by merit of the activities that take place within their walls. These are the rooms of our homes that see a lot of action—kitchens, bathrooms, home offices, and double-duty spaces that accommodate a number of functions at the same time. To be effective, the storage in these areas must be ample, flexible, accessible, and strategically positioned—which means that many different kinds of storage will be necessary in the same room.

The very framework of each of these rooms holds vast potential for those enterprising enough to mine all of the opportunities they offer. After tackling the obvious spaces, take a careful look behind doors, under and between windows, between shelves, under stairs, in corners, and so on. Most of us have plenty of unused space waiting to be reclaimed. For instance, if there is sufficient space between the items stored on a shelf and the shelf above it, install hanging wire baskets. Or turn the width of the wall between two windows, or under them, into shelves. If there you have six or more inches behind an open door, slip in narrow shelves, or build triangularly shaped shelves in a wasted corner. Make the most of every square inch so these hard-working spaces are as efficient and accommodating as possible.

opposite
A variety of different options can coexist in the same room, and offer a range of storage solutions—including some that are quite decorative. Rustic vintage cupboards with see-through doors can be installed on walls instead of traditional cabinets; molding can be used to forge ledges to hold pretty serving pieces; and built-in cabinetry can be faced with an ornamental facade such as beadboard.

right
Ideally, a washroom or bathroom should incorporate as much built-in storage as possible to make the most efficient use of available space. However, in smaller spaces it is necessary to think creatively. Here, virtually every available square inch is devoted to cabinetry. To compensate for a lack of open wall space, the towel rack is hung on the side of the vanity.

KITCHENS Like the hearth of yesteryear, today's kitchen is the heart of a home—and every family member uses it at some point. Thus, the functions performed in this space are many and varied. Depending on the size and scope of the kitchen, it can be used as a dining area, home office, craft area, playroom, and social center throughout the day. This can make it the busiest room in a residence, and as such, it needs to be carefully planned, executed, and organized.

Most kitchen storage is usually built-in, floor-to-ceiling cabinetry, split in the center to accommodate continuous countertops used as work surfaces. The beauty of this system is that these cabinets hold all and hide all as needed. If fronted with see-through doors, they can also show all in a decorative fashion. Plus, there are a wide range of interior fittings that can be used to customize them, such as drawers, dividers, shelves, racks and carousels, or special features that can be integrated into their design, such as pullout components and chopping blocks.

Unfitted kitchens, comprised of various types of freestanding storage, offer another storage option and allow great flexibility for those who like to rearrange their surroundings or move frequently. They also provide a wider range of options in terms of décor, since these pieces can range from contemporary to antique. The entire kitchen can become eclectic yet remain an efficient environment with this approach. For instance, a large antique Welch dresser can be laden with accouterments, leaving the rest of the kitchen relatively free from clutter.

Regardless of which type of kitchen one opts to install, there are some basic storage rules to observe and many other ways to coax storage spaces out of this room. Start by situating items near the locations in the room where they are most often used, then determining what sort of storage best suits their needs.

opposite
Storage that keeps everything in order and out of the way is the key to success in the kitchen. Easy-access systems such as hanging pot racks, wall-mounted plate racks, and open shelves increase the odds of keeping order since they are so convenient and easy to reach.

above left
Store cooking equipment, utensils, and ingredients that you use all the time within easy reach. Here, some cleverly conceived solutions, such as a ledge surrounding the cooking hood, a rack over the burner, and built-in shelves next to the oven, allow everything necessary to be close at hand.

above right
Commercial inserts come in myriad incarnations and are the ideal way to make the most optimal use of the space on shelves and organize cooking supplies.

Store appliances, cookware, and tableware as close as possible to the workstations or activity areas where they are needed. Then make sure storage options are used to their maximum potential. Fortunately, the options are endless these days thanks to the profusion of available storage products. Many are specifically made to be used for certain tasks and as such, offer novel new ways to address storage issues. For instance, there is a vast range of baskets and racks for kitchen tools and utensils alone. Backs of doors can be fitted with shelves, racks, or grids; overhead racks suspended from ceilings can hold pots and pans; the bottoms of hanging cabinets can be fitted with hooks or holders for wine glasses, spice racks, or utensils; or walls can be hung with grids or hooks for all sorts of items. But all of these techniques demand heavy-duty grounding, or the weight of kitchen equipment will pull them out of walls. And they also require heavy-duty vigilance, since they will only be effective if they are used at all times.

> **All About** Cabinets

Cabinets are one of the most functional forms of storage, especially since they keep everything hidden away and protected from dust and grime. Better yet, they come in such a wide range of decorative options that they can be used virtually anywhere in the home, be it hard-working spaces like the kitchen, family room, bathroom, basement, or home office, or showrooms such as the living room and dining areas.

But we rarely choose cabinets purely for function alone—especially since they can bring an aesthetic cache to a home that can also up its style quotient and resale value. But knowing what to look for and where to use them can be confusing, especially considering the fact that the options are literally endless. Thanks to the custom cabinetry industry, if you can't find what you want you can have it made to your wants and needs. However, in making choices, there are a number of issues to consider.

> **Custom Versus Prefabricated Cabinets** Custom-made cabinets can be quite expensive, but can also optimize space since they will be built to fill every available square inch. They may also last longer, have a better warranty, and grant more decorative options to homeowners. But pre-manufactured cabinets can look and work just as well, and can be coupled with custom-made units for the nooks and crannies that can't be mined with what is available on the market. The decision to use one or the other should be based on the budget spent on an entire room or home so the costs for the project are proportionate to the rest of the structural components in your home.

> **Construction** Particleboard or plywood shelves inside cabinets are sturdier than solid wood because they are less apt to warp. Interior shelves should be at least 1/2 (1.3cm) to 5/8 (1.5cm) inches thick so they don't bow under the weight of what's on them. The front, back, and sides

above
Custom-made cabinets are often the most practical option in a kitchen since they are constructed to fit the space and utilize every available square inch. They can also be made in any decorative style, or sans doors to provide display for favorite items.

should be at least $\frac{3}{4}$ inch (1.9cm) thick to sturdily contain shelves and all that is on them. Wooden drawers that are dovetailed at corners rather than stapled will hold up better over time.

> Size Custom cabinets can be made in any size and shape. Stock cabinets come in 3-inch (7.6cm) increments. When installing cabinets, one of the biggest decisions to make is whether to build them all the way to the ceiling, which yields the most storage space and an orderly, trim appearance, or whether to leave a soffit above cabinets for display purposes. There are plusses and minuses for either approach. While those extra-high cabinets can be hard to reach, anything put on display in a soffit can become quite dusty.

> Finishes and Detailing Three quarters of the cost will be determined by the finish employed on the cabinet and detailing. Economical choices include laminates, certain woods (such as maple), and medium-density wrapped fiberboard, while pricier options include spray lacquers,

polyester finishes, beveled-glass inserts, and certain woods, veneers, and decorative treatments (such as cherry, walnut, mahogany, or antiqued finishes). Raised panels and molding add to the cost of cabinets, but will also substantially increase their decorative cache.

> Interior Hardware Even though they don't show, it's critical not to skimp on the fittings that keep cabinets in good working order. The best hinges keep doors aligned, are partly or totally concealed, adjust in every direction, and are made of a sturdy metal such as chrome, nickel, or brass. Sturdy drawer glides are also important to keep all components of a cabinet system in good working order. They should be under- or side-mounted and made of a sturdy metal with ball bearings.

> Exterior Hardware Choices abound for knobs and pulls these days, and for good reason. These have become the proverbial icing on the cake when it comes to cabinetry and can make prosaic pieces remarkable. They are

made by manufacturers and artisans in myriad materials and every imaginable decorative style. But prices also vary across the board, and costs can add up. For instance, some pulls or knobs can cost upwards of $30 each; multiply that by enough for an entire room of cabinets and you're looking at hundreds of dollars.

> Interior Fittings Today, everything from fancy utensil trays and spice racks to rollout shelves and pop-up appliance platforms can be used to outfit cabinetry, but every extra adds to the final budget. Fittings to improve convenience should not be forgotten, but must be carefully planned out. Splurge on the things you will really use and don't succumb to fittings you won't—no matter how engaging they may seem.

> How Much to Build You can never have too much storage. If you are building cabinetry from scratch, designers advise you to build about one-third more than necessary to accommodate growing needs.

right
Built-ins give you the leeway to tailor cabinets specifically to your needs. Here, two extra-tall cabinet banks house pullout drawers that flank a vanity and sink in a bathroom.

right
There is no wasted space in this bank of built-in cabinets. Even the closet doors are put to good use with blackboards for grocery lists and messages.

WASHROOMS AND BATHROOMS Standing at a sink and washing, shaving, brushing teeth, or applying makeup illustrates how critical appropriate and accessible storage is in these spaces. The same holds true when showering or bathing. You need immediate and easy access to a range of essentials, including soap, a razor, a toothbrush, toiletries, and towels. Most sinks, showers, and baths are surrounded with surfaces to hold some of these items, built-in alcoves or cabinets to hold the rest, and towel racks or hooks are nearby. But managing the storage situation in a bathroom doesn't stop there, since there are a range of special tools one needs to properly store toiletries, such as toothbrush holders and soap dishes, that are also requisites in this room.

Fortunately, bathrooms seem to have more square footage than ever before. Many of these larger spaces incorporate sizable sink areas or expansive vanities with ample storage underneath, or have whole walls devoted to built-in storage. And there are also a range of cabinets and chests available today that are specially designed for this room and can be used to pick up the overflow if floor space permits.

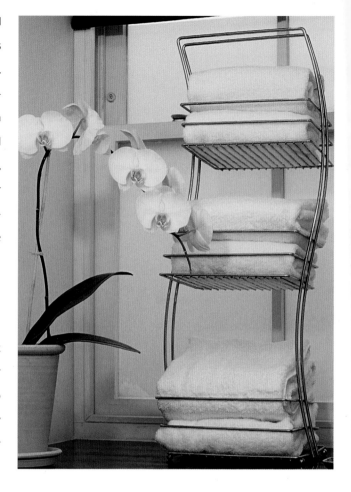

But regardless of size, the storage over sinks should be at eye level to allow easy access to necessities; hooks, bars, or racks for towels should be installed near sinks, showers, and tubs; and extra rolls of toilet paper should be stored near toilets. A cabinet under a basin is also a very pragmatic use of space, since it can conceal pipes and provide a good chunk of concealed, accessible storage. And there are many different holders that can be used to add extra nooks for storing supplies for bathtubs or showers that lack them. Special racks can be stretched across the widths of bathtubs or hung from showerheads.

Integrating storage into smaller bathrooms can be more challenging, but is viable with ingenuity and planning. It is possible to "pull" space from almost nowhere—such as adding alcoves on to the ends or sides of tubs for towel storage, placing small cabinets or chests under open basins or where open floor space permits, adding shelving over toilets, and installing corner shelves.

above
The right wire towel rack can turn a window ledge over a bathtub into a source of strategically located storage.

right
Sleek cabinets surrounding a pedestal sink are equipped with baskets that slide out instead of doors, which makes it easier to access towels.

DOUBLE-DUTY SPACES Some say the formal living room is on the way out. Or that the dining room is dead. And for good reason—today's versions of these rooms, and others in a home such as the kitchen, library, bedroom, and den often combine functions that in the past would merit an entire room of their own. But few of us have the luxury to devote a whole room to a single pursuit. Space constraints in general, coupled with contemporary styles of design, have led to the rise of double-duty spaces or rooms in every part of the home.

left top

All the equipment related to a home office can be safe from prying eyes when it is kept behind closed doors. By tapping into an attractive hidden system, a workspace can blend into a double-duty space. Behind the doors, this compact home office utilizes every available space efficiently. The chair can be stored next to the bookcase when not in use.

left bottom

A wraparound counter can make the transition from one space to another by incorporating different types of storage. In the kitchen area, cabinets hide pots and pans, but in the family room, open shelving makes CDs and tapes easy to reach for constant use.

Ironically, rooms devoted solely to one purpose were a luxury when they were first developed in the seventeenth century, and are a luxury once again today for those who live in smaller or crowded quarters. But this quandary forces us to think creatively, especially where storage is concerned. It can be challenging and rewarding to reclaim an under-utilized space in a home.

The best kinds of combined spaces require careful planning and implementation in order to really work. Flexibility and well-planned storage is the key to success, especially if space is at a premium. For instance, a living or dining room that also sports a home office should have ample concealed storage to accommodate all required accouterments. The same is true of a family room with a study or art area for kids or a kitchen that harbors a craft or hobby center.

But the most important aspect of a double-duty space is the existence of some sort of structural device to separate the functions in a room when necessary, especially since some tasks performed in a double-duty space tend to encroach on other functions in a room. If papers are strewn all over a desk in a living or dining area, the space is less likely to be used for entertaining or eating. And it can be impossible to go to bed in a room where work is out and beckoning you to do it. This divider or screening system should be easy to employ so the space can be quickly converted back and forth.

HOME OFFICES Whether you have a whole room to devote to a home office, or must make the most of a shared or found space, most working spaces start out very differently than they end up. First comes a simple desk or work surface, equipped with a phone and a computer. Next come a printer, fax, and copy machine. Before long, files crowd the floor or supplies consume the space in a slapdash fashion.

For home offices, storage solutions run the gamut from cabinets, shelves, and even workstations-cum-armoires that conceal whole offices behind their doors for shared spaces, to extensive systems that are designed for both the residential and contract markets. In all cases, these pieces are not meant to re-create a commercial office at home, but rather to personally tailor a working environment to an individual's working habits and storage needs without having to consider the dictates of anyone else.

There are many ways to do this, but in all cases home offices—especially those that are on the small side or orchestrated as part of a double-duty space—need to be very functional domains. Forethought must be given to the way they are used and organized. Whether you choose a decorative desk or a practical, no-nonsense workstation, it needs to be efficiently configured and offer enough storage to accommodate your equipment, supplies, and papers. At the least, it is safe to assume that virtually every home office will have to house a computer, printer, phone, fax, files, and minimal supplies, but some may require an extensive spread, complete with a workstation to house another user, a conference table for meetings, and a extensive storage options for files and books.

Built-ins that are custom made for a space or setups that are pieced together from a pre-fabricated or component system offer optimal solutions for creating a workspace that meets individual needs. Both types of systems can be tailored to any specific area, fabricated in many materials, and fashioned in dozens of different decorative styles. They can also be used to make the space comfortable, accommodating, and attractive at the same time. Plus, small spaces benefit greatly with systems that can be used to make the most of every available square inch. If configured properly, these systems can often make a space seem larger than its actual square footage.

Individual office components can also be used to create a home office, and offer a bit more decorative leeway. A wide range of furnishings appropriate for the home office exist today executed in many decorative styles. However, it is also possible to tailor a space to your own taste. An antique table used as a desk, baskets substituted for filing cabinets, and idiosyncratic chests used in lieu of cabinets can all offer the same utility as the furnishings that were intended for these tasks, but will have a more ornamental impact on the environment.

Bottom line, making the most sense of these areas, regardless of whether they are "compact" or "stolen" spaces and quite small or a whole room, takes planning and creativity. After all, the trappings and materials of a work environment can quickly grow to fill whatever space we allot to this task.

above
A home office can grow to fill the space you have to devote to it. But by using furnishings on wheels, the space can be quickly rearranged to accommodate other activities.

above
Economical, readymade components were pieced together to create this compact home office for two, which has everything needed to fulfill the requirements of its users. Best of all, the parts can be easily reconfigured if and when this family's needs change.

right
A compact and efficient workstation makes a small space go a long way. Shelves add more storage space and can also be devoted to other uses when and if the workstation is moved to another section of the home.

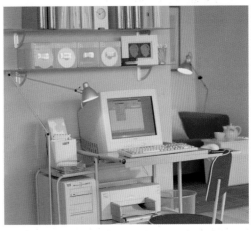

KIDS' SPACES Anyone with children knows that their wants and needs are quite different than adults, and the spaces or rooms they use must be carefully configured to accommodate these needs. For instance, cleaning up does not come naturally to kids, and unless their spaces are strategically conceived and executed, they may leave everything out in a messy and exasperating jumble. Also, adults and kids must often co-habit the same room, and this also calls for some juggling to balance the needs of both age groups.

Wherever children will be stationed in a space, it is critical to plan storage that will not only accommodate their possessions, but will also be both physically accessible to them and attractive enough to encourage them to put away their possessions.

For bulky items, consider colorful baskets or bins. For clothes, opt for interesting solutions, such as pretty hangers for girls or bright metal storage lockers for boys. Avoid deep drawers and shelves since they offer up too much space at once. They can become very messy and be too large for a child to access, while shallow ones are easier to keep in order. Cabinets should be easily accessible, which means they should be set or built at lower heights rather than higher ones. But high shelves do come in handy for older children who want to show off prized possessions or keep them out of the grasp of younger siblings. Also, shelves should always be adjustable to allow for the changing needs of growing children, whose tastes quickly become more sophisticated as the years go by. Before long, kids will opt for audio-visual equipment and stereo systems rather than toys, and ideally, the same storage system should be able to accommodate both types of items.

above

Find a place to stash away toys and supplies for children in every space they use, even if it's only a drawer or a makeshift area with a chest or two. This way, children can play or color wherever they happen to be, and there is a place to put their possessions away with some sense of order.

left

Cabinets and shelves used together offer children a way to store a variety of items, and offer opportunities to segregate and organize items. Low cabinets can hide bulky or unattractive items that don't match the decor, but keep them well within reach for little kids.

> **Organizing** and Storing Books

Many of us have substantial accumulations of books, but we don't give much thought to how we position, organize, and store them. Books need to be organized and stored in a style that befits your home decor and reading habits. We tend to put them in one place in our homes, yet there may be comfortable places to read established in many different rooms. We also usually organize them in a relatively haphazard way, which can make it difficult to find specific titles when we want to retrieve them. And few of us realize that books require a certain environment if they are expected to stand the test of time. If you want to keep them for posterity, thought must be given to the environmental conditions in your home.

> Choosing Bookshelves

Appearance and cost usually come first when buying bookshelves, but it is also important to consider the size, weight, and number of books you have to shelve. A collection of paperback books doesn't demand a stately, sizable, or particularly strong set of shelves, but oversized art, decorating, and gardening books do. Consider different kinds of shelving for books in each room of your home. Knockdown or collapsable units with several shelves should do for paperbacks, while sturdy units with shelves that are at least 12 inches (30 cm) deep and 15 inches (38 cm) high will be necessary for hefty or oversized volumes.

> Ready-Made Bookshelves

Though some ready-made units require some assembly, most are meant to be brought home and put to work immediately. They are less expensive than built-ins, but cover a wide spectrum, ranging from inexpensive knockdowns to exquisitely crafted pieces that can be considered fine furniture. Economical choices include shelving units made of

fiberboard or particleboard, laminates, lighter gauge metal, and veneers. They can often have snap-together joints that can loosen if they are moved often, so use care with these shelves. Higher-end pieces are made of plywood covered with wood veneers, solid wood, or high gauge metal. These are sturdier and have hardware or fittings that are better able to stand the tests of weight and time.

> **Custom-Made Bookshelves** The biggest advantage to custom shelving is that it can be made to fit any space and accommodate items of any size. They can be built-in or freestanding; crafted to match a certain décor or deco-

rative style; and take advantage of every inch of space in a setting. But they will also be more expensive than the store-bought alternatives, and it may be necessary to monitor the building process for this type of shelving.

> **Siting Bookshelves** Regardless of whether they're store-bought or custom-made, bookshelves must be sited in a spot that will properly support the load. Shelves that are meant to hold extremely heavy loads should be positioned along a perimeter weight-bearing wall in a room, not a section of drywall. Bookshelves that are more than 4 feet (122 cm) high should be equipped with anti-topple

devices. These can include adjustable feet, shims (thin pieces of wood that are used under the feet to level shelves), and anchors that attach shelves to walls.

> **Determining Linear Footage** While it is hard to be exact, it is important to have an idea of how many linear feet of shelving are needed to store a collection of books. Stack all the books a shelving unit is meant to accommodate, and measure them in groups. Then overbuild. Some like the look of empty shelves, but most of us tend to amass more and more. Plus, more space gives you the option of integrating collectibles into the mix.

> **Putting Books Away** Like items in your home, place books where they are used. The mystery novels you read at night in the study or den don't belong with the art books you have on view in your living room; cookbooks belong in the kitchen; and reference books should be situated where you or the kids work on projects and assignments. Also keep in mind that bookshelves aren't the only option. Books can be stacked on tables, mantels, and even the floor if the spot is out-of-the-way and safe from trampling.

> **Organizing Books** Given that shelves are varying heights, it pays to group books according to size to conserve on storage space.

Besides the fact that placing small books next to large ones is an inefficient use of space, this will also cause their covers to splay. For this reason, books should be firmly supported by neighboring books or bookends to prevent them from warping or fraying. Instead, categorize books first by size and then subcategorize them by subject, genre, and author. Other options include shelving paperbacks and hardcovers in separate locations and storing valuable, antique, or prized books in shelves with glass doors. Make sure any shelving system has enough depth to leave room for air to flow behind books, since damp air can cause mold.

> **Caring for Books** If you want your books to last, they need to be stored in a cool, dry environment. Since this isn't always possible, do the next best thing: avoid putting them where there are extreme swings in temperature, humidity, and lighting conditions, and keep them dust-free. The temperature in a room should stay between 65 and 70 degrees and the relative humidity should be about 50 percent. To keep books from abrading, fading, or becoming brittle, they should be dusted frequently (dust is abrasive) and kept away from direct sunlight and the heat of radiators and fireplaces.

> **Organizing** Your Stuff

Clever storage solutions and ideas
for the way you really live.

above
Eliminate the jumble of different-sized jars and containers with a perfectly sized spice rack. Usefulness and practicality aren't the only considerations; seek items designed to show off the beauty of what is stored within.

above
Use little boxes in a variety of sizes to organize a desktop or pullout drawer. Perfect for art supplies, hardware, jewelry—and especially good in kitchens, where they complement the hardworking look of appliances and fixtures.

above
Hanging rack systems can accommodate a number of different-size utensils thanks to a variety of unique attachments. They are also practical additions for efficiency—placing needed items in view and close at hand.

__above
Perfect for keeping often-used cooking tools within
easy reach, a kitchen worktable can increase your efficiency and offer up more storage. A large unit can
nearly double the amount of workspace and storage
space for tight quarters.

right

Forget desktops littered with outdated notes. Keep little slips of paper from getting misplaced or lost with a message-go-round. This is about as simple an organizing system as they come, but extremely effective for its size and shape.

right

It's easy to prioritize mail, bills, tickets, and more with a holder that has individual openings. Choose storage like this to suit your habits—even the best file storage idea won't work if you are a "piles of paper" worker, and not a "put it in folders" type.

right

Until the "paper free" office becomes more common, there will always be filing to do. But, work spaces do not have to be defined by file drawers. Organize files, letters, and records in one unit that can easily expand as your needs do.

above

Stacking boxes and metal chests with the same industrial demeanor can help organize items in a variety of hard-working spaces. Add labels for quick identification, and keep in mind that this system can be as decorative as it is practical.

above top

A cabinet with open and closed storage can be used, moved, or stowed away anywhere in a home thanks to its wheels. Ergonomic as well as practical, items remain in easy reach.

above bottom

You may not want the look or the fixed nature of a corporate office if you are working at home: File cabinets on wheels let you move a home office wherever you want to do some work. They tuck away easily into a corner or closet when not in use.

All Around the House

Planning storage for the main living areas in our homes is an obvious endeavor that we all do by second nature. There are systems and pieces that are made in every incarnation to address the needs we have in these specific rooms. But recognizing that there are many other parts of a home to organize or adapt in the same way is the final step to addressing storage concerns—especially if your household inventory requires even more storage than the space you seemingly have permits.

It is surprising where one can find valuable recesses of storage space. There are so many areas in our residences we can use for storage, and it is critical to make the most of them. Attics and basements, storage lockers in apartments or condominiums, extra-large hallways and landings, the spaces under stairs or eaves, mudrooms or utility rooms, and oversized garages or storage sheds offer up vast expanses that can be turned into major sources of storage with proper planning and implementation.

However, the decision to utilize these spaces is usually born of demand and availability, which prompts a different approach than in other areas of the home. Chances are you won't set out to equip these spaces with custom built-ins or beautifully crafted pieces of furniture. You may realize that in some instances, built-ins will optimize available space, but for the most part these are the areas in your home where improvisation may become your modus operandi. Done well, the results are just as efficient and effective.

opposite
Valuable recesses of storage and display can be found in unlikely spots, such as this spacious foyer. Beautiful built-ins that incorporate cabinets and shelves make this a prime and productive source of storage.

above
Shelves should preferably
be adjustable, and there are
several systems to use that
accomplish this. The hole-
and-peg system uses little
hardware and can easily be
reconfigured as your needs
change.

> **Shelving** Considerations

Should you buy a shelving system or
have one built in? There are no standard sizes when
it comes to your possessions, and fortunately, there are
many self-assembled shelving systems on the market that
can be adjusted to allow you to accommodate undersized or
oversized items. But there's only so much flexibility a prefab-
ricated system can offer. If you build for yourself, you can customize your shelving unit to fit your possessions to a tee.
Regardless of which system you choose, following are some
factors you should keep in mind.

> **Flexibility** Because your storage
needs change as you gain and
lose possessions, shelves should
be adjustable. There are several
basic systems to choose from. In
hole-and-peg systems (also
called slot-and-dowel), shelves
rest on pegs plugged into holes
in the sides of a unit; strip-and-
clip uses the same principle, but
features metal strips attached to
the side walls of a unit with
metal clips that can be inserted
into the strips to hold the
shelves; and rail-and-bracket systems use vertical tracks, or rails,
attached directly to the wall,
with brackets inserted into these
rails to hold shelves. Hole-and-
peg systems are suitable for
short shelf spans and require little hardware, which makes them
ideal for glass shelves and display
units. Strip-and-clip systems are
the most flexible and can support shelves that are a bit heavier. Rail-and-bracket systems are
adequate for larger spans and
heavier loads, and work well in
utilitarian sites.

> **Sizes and Spans** The load a shelf
can hold depends on the material it's made of, its thickness, and
the span between supports. For
short shelves, a support at either
end is adequate, but long shelves
require intermediate supports.
Heaver loads also demand shorter spans between supports. In
general, shelves for light loads
can be as slim as $\frac{1}{4}$ inch (6 mm)
thick, but shelves for heavy
things should always be at least
$\frac{3}{4}$ inch (1.9 cm) thick and preferably 1 inch (2.5 cm) thick with
longer spans; anything less will
eventually sag. Spans can exceed

32 inches (81 cm) with the proper support, but it is not recommended. When you go over this length, the weight of the shelf itself can cause it to sag.

> **Materials** Medium-density fiberboard, which is also called particleboard, is cheap, sturdy, doesn't warp as much as solid wood, can be easily cut into shapes, and comes in many thicknesses. However, it does require a finish to mask its appearance. Also, it tends to be heavier than other materials (such as plywood and wood) so particleboard shelves should not have long spans. Melamine-faced board is cheap, easy to clean, relatively waterproof, and strong, which makes it ideal for use in utility areas. A drawback is that its edges are susceptible to chipping and it can look cheap. Plywood is cheaper than wood, extremely strong, comes in waterproof varieties, can be veneered with other woods, and is quite attractive on its own. However, it can also look cheap and the edges can be susceptible to dents and chips. Most types of wood are also suitable to craft into shelving, but can be much more expensive and heavy than plywood with wood veneers. Metals, ranging from stainless steel to wrought iron, are also used for shelves, but lighter gauges will not be appropriate for heavy loads.

FOYERS, LANDINGS, AND HALLWAYS Foyers, landings, and hallways, are found spaces. They're often expansive enough to accommodate a wide variety of storage options, yet are often overlooked as sources of storage. Consider a grand entry foyer in a traditional home, built long before spacious closets were the norm. Instead of making structural changes to the space, furnish the foyer with a spacious armoire to add more storage for outerwear. Or scale down to a compact cabinet, cupboard, chest, or bench with storage concealed under its seat for hats, scarves, gloves, and boots. If there's enough room, the pieces you install in the foyer can also pick up the slack from other, more crowded rooms short on storage spaces. There's no reason why a large cabinet can't harbor dishes or large serving pieces that won't fit in the dining room.

Hallways, landings, and the triangular spaces under stairs are ideal for built-in or set-in storage systems. Hallways that connect rooms are fairly narrow and need to remain a certain width. At the same time, hallways that flank landings and stairs usually take some twists and turns, or incorporate alcoves and recesses. And the spaces under stairs are oddly shaped nooks and crannies. For these reasons, all accommodate built-in storage systems fairly unobtrusively, especially since this type of storage makes the most efficient use of available space. For example, an entire library can be lodged on one side of a wide staircase or line a sizable second- or third-floor landing. Or a whole home office or spacious closet can be fitted under the stairs.

above
Even a small foyer can accommodate built-ins if they are configured correctly. A shallow unit lines the wall that flanks the door to this apartment, and looks out over a broader passageway into the living area.

opposite
Make a wall of built-in storage closets in a narrow hallway blend in by fabricating them in a material that mimics the structural underpinnings of your home. This wall of closets faced in wood panels and trimmed with elegant pulls seems more decorative than functional thanks to its design, yet yields a large amount of storage space.

> Keeping Clothing
Closets in Shape

Half the battle of getting dressed in the morning is picking out the pieces of your outfit. While you don't need expensive closet organizers, you do have to arrange clothing and accessories so they're visible, accessible, and make proper use of available space.

> **Don't Overload Closets** Garments should not be crammed together because this will cause wrinkling and keep air from circulating around them to eliminate odors. Proper storage tactics prolong the life of a wardrobe.

> **Change Wardrobes** Twice a year (ideally at benchmark holidays such as Labor Day and Memorial Day), change or rearrange your wardrobe closets by breaking out, reevaluating, weeding through, and rearranging all your clothes.

> **Pare Down** Fashion stylists agree that winnowing your wardrobe once or twice a year makes it more wearable. The best time is when you change over wardrobes. Try everything on and get rid of the things that don't look good on you, don't fit properly, don't go with anything else you own, or haven't been worn in more than a year.

> **Categorize Your Pieces** Hang or group items by category in your closet, then sub-divide them by color, season, or both. Matching outfits can be hung together or separated by piece. The first approach makes it easy to grab a complete "uniform" in the morning, but can also stifle creativity. Separating matching outfits can force you to see your pieces in new ways and stretch your wardrobe.

> **Use Proper Hangers** Suit jackets should be hung on thicker, contoured hangers so the collar and shoulders will break properly and their shaping won't become distorted. Avoid wire hangers altogether because they rust, which can damage clothing. If you are short on space, consider multiple hangers that stack four or five garments in a ladder-like configuration for blouses, pants, and skirts.

> Use Cloth Storage Bags Remove all plastic covers from your clothes when they are returned from the dry cleaners and don't hang clothes in plastic garment bags; they trap moisture that can encourage mildew or yellow clothes. Instead, use cloth storage bags to shield out-of-season clothes, or make your own with cotton sheets or pillowcases (which are particularly effective for suit jackets and skirts).

> Shelve the Knits Whatever their fiber content, knits should never be hung or they will stretch out of shape. Fold them and arrange them by type, fiber, and color on shelves where they can be seen. For instance, make separate stacks for cotton t-shirts, cotton turtlenecks, wool sweaters, and so on. Leave some space for air circulation between the top of a stack and the shelf above it.

> Categorize Shoes Shoes should be organized by style and color, and boxes should be clearly labeled so you know what you have. Use clear plastic shoeboxes or put Polaroid photos on cardboard ones. If you don't have room for shoeboxes, which do take up lots of space, use fabric or mesh shoe bags (leather has to breathe so plastic can be a problem).

> Arrange Accessories Everything else, from scarves and ties to handbags and jewelry, should also be stored properly so you can access it when dressing. The key is to see what you have; otherwise you will forget about it. To do this, use special hangers that display ties and scarves; put jewelry in clear plastic tackle boxes or hanging makeup bags; and store socks and underwear in mesh baskets or clear plastic boxes on closet shelves.

ALL ABOUT CLOSETS Closets are the unsung heroes of the home since they hold more than their fair share of possessions and can accommodate virtually anything—depending on how they are arranged. They keep things out of sight and are relatively organized since they are comprised of a variety of structural elements, such as rods, shelves, drawers, bins, baskets, and cubbies.

So what type of closet should you choose? There is no such thing as the ideal closet. They are as individual as their owners and the possessions they hold. But can be classed into two different categories—wall closets or walk-ins. Wall closets are usually approximately 24 inches (61 cm) deep and eat up far less floor space than walk-ins, which makes them a good option in rooms that are tight on space. They are also very efficient, economical to build, and easy to equip thanks to their straightforward configuration. Walk-ins come in every size and configuration, with some as large as a small room.

In fitting out the various types of closets that exist, anything goes as long as it makes the most of a space. Many closets are outfitted with expensive built-ins that sport special fittings and utilize every square inch of space, while others are sensibly arranged with economical wire systems that combine hanging fixtures, shelves, and stacking baskets that are just as effective and easier to adapt to changing needs.

above
Wall closets usually eat up far less floor space than walk-ins, which makes them the best option for smaller rooms. They are also easier to outfit with store-bought or built-in fittings due to their straightforward configuration.

above
A walk-in closet can be so expansive that it approximates the dimensions of a whole room. By equipping it with a sofa, it becomes a bona fide dressing room.

Narrower shelves are preferable in a linen closet, since they make it easier to maintain order. Widely spaced shelves encourage high, heavy stacks of linens that can be difficult to negotiate when it's time to remove something.

When equipping a wardrobe closet, it is important to remember that clothing, especially women's apparel, comes in a wide range of lengths and requires a variety of different hangers. Consequently, all rods installed in a closet should be adjustable. Ideally, the supports used to anchor them to a wall should mimic those used for adjustable shelving so they can be raised and lowered when necessary to accommodate pants, shirts, dresses, or skirts. If you are short on storage space, consider using the very top part of your closet for seasonal items. It is usually dead space, and cardboard storage boxes set on their sides can serve as adequate makeshift shelves. Don't forget to invest in a sturdy step stool that can be kept nearby. Also remember that extra-large closets can double as dressing rooms if there is an area in the middle in which one can move around.

Unlike clothing closets, linen closets are fairly straightforward affairs that are outfitted with shelves. Narrow and closely spaced shelves are preferable to deep and distantly spaced ones for several reasons. It is easier to see what you have on narrow shelves. Widely spaced shelves encourage high, heavy stacks of linens that can be heavy or cumbersome to negotiate when you need to remove something from the pile and smaller piles encourage better air circulation. The classic method of stacking linens and towels is to place freshly laundered items on the bottom of a pile to encourage you to rotate the pieces in use. Sets should be stacked together so all of the pieces will age at the same rate.

> Closet 411

Here's how to make the most of the closets in your home and keep them in good shape.

> Air Care The closets in your home should be cool, dry, and have adequate air circulation since mildew can grow in warm, humid conditions and affect both the items you have in storage and the closet's shelves and walls (especially if made of wood). This means that items should not be overcrowded and jammed into shelves or onto hanging rails. Also, the door to a closet should be left open periodically to allow fresh air to circulate.

> Periodic Cleanups All closets need to be cleaned out at least once a year by emptying them out, washing and dusting down shelves, baseboards, and walls, and letting all the surfaces dry thoroughly before returning items to storage. Also make sure the garments or linens you put back in a closet are clean and dry.

> Evicting Critters It is critical to periodically check all closets thoroughly for insects, and eliminate them if they are present. Linen closets should be cleaned at least once a year, but it is preferable to make sure clothing closets are critter-free before you break out your wardrobe for a new season, which usually amounts to twice a year. In either case, take everything out of the closet and wipe down all surfaces, including baseboards, with soap and water. And don't forget to give cedar closets this treatment; even though most insects will not seek out a cedar environment, once you introduce an item that has larvae in it, they can flourish just as well in cedar as anywhere else.

Think about your needs before outfitting a closet. Kids require spaces of different sizes, racks hung at low heights, and bins to hold bulky things.

> Moth Prevention Tactics Linens and clothes that have been packed away in moth balls for any amount of time need to be "prepped" when you break them out of storage and put them back into an actively used closet. Inspect them to make sure they are indeed larvae-free, and air them out until they have no odor. The best place to do this is outside in the shade. Length of time will depend on strength of odor.

> Inventory Everything Take photographs or a video of all or your closets in case there's a fire or a flood. Most of us have far more clothing, accessories, and linens than we realize, and can never really remember what we own. For that reason, be careful to document every closet in your home, methodically committing every shelf, rack, and basket to film.

> Think Ahead Accommodating what you already own is only half the battle when you set up the closet systems in your home. Think about what your needs will be in the future and how much space those needs will require. If you have a growing family, your linen closet will obviously need to hold more and you will also have to provide closet space for children. Your needs may also change, and unless you are committed to pruning the items in your wardrobe that are little used you will soon need a larger home.

UTILITY ROOMS, MUDROOMS, AND LAUNDRY ROOMS

These spaces are often neglected in a home. It is considered the norm—especially in residences with several children—to spot piles of muddy boots and soccer shoes in a jumble on the floor of the suburban mudroom, or jackets heaped in mounds on only a few hooks. And bins of linens and clothes stacked up on the floor in the typical laundry room are an ordinary sight to most. But instead of letting these spaces become clutter zones, use them to their potential.

Although mudrooms and utility rooms are attached to a residence, they are usually treated as spaces that don't rate on the neatness scale we apply to other rooms in our homes. But since these areas get a lot of wear and tear, it makes the most sense to opt for cost-effective storage systems here.

Start with lots of hooks for jackets and coats, and a bench with a lift-up seat for boots and shoes. From there, add cubbies or cabinets for sports equipment, backpacks, and other items you want to accommodate here. Consider specialized storage items such as racks for holding boots and shoes or scarves and hats.

Organizing the laundry room is more critical than it seems. Besides enough room to accommodate the washer and dryer, which take up a substantial amount of space, some other mandatory require-ments include counter space for folding clothes, storage space for washing supplies, and floor space for an ironing board and fold-up drying rack. The washer and dryer must be situated in the space so their doors can be easily opened and closed, and so they are conve-niently accessible for repairs. If space is at a premium, storage cab-inets for supplies can be built in above these appliances, an ironing board and folding counters can swing down from the wall, and fold-up rolling hampers can be used to sort and store wash as it is being done.

_**above top**
A mudroom should not always be treated like a sec-ond-class citizen in our homes. We should apply the same neatness scale to this area as we do to out other rooms, and outfit it with trappings that increase its efficiency, such as a bench for putting on boots, pegs for coats, and baskets for bulky items.

_**above bottom**
Storage cabinets for supplies increase the utility of a laundry room. Supplies are always on hand right where they're needed, yet neatly stashed away behind closed doors. A hanging rod also keeps ironed shirts in shape.

_**opposite**
Opt for sturdy, cost-effective storage systems in utility rooms to keep them in good organizational shape. Here, metal shelves turn a utility room into overflow storage for staples and sets of glasses and dishes.

above
A freestanding shelving unit can assume all the elegance of a
built-in unit with the right decorative approach. A crown molding
adds sophistication to the design of this unit, which is squeezed
into such a tight space that it mimics a built-in. The elegant
antique volumes and upscale periodicals that fill the unit round
out its cultivated demeanor.

opposite
Readymade shelving units have a number of advantages. They can be put to work immediately; are
portable; and if more are needed it's easy to go out and
buy another one that is exactly the same as the first.

> **All About** Shelves

Whether freestanding or built-in, the most versatile form of storage is a set of shelves. Shelves can usually be adjusted to accommodate items of various sizes and weights. Smaller items can be stored on them stacked in bins. They can be used in every room of your home and they come in countless incarnations. When buying shelves, appearance and cost are usually the first issues we consider, yet there are many other issues to assess first.

> **How Big Should They Be?** Think about the size, weight, and number of objects you want to store on a set of shelves. This will affect the height, depth, and width of the shelves, and determine how strong, sturdy, and stable they need to be.

> **Where Will They Be Used?** Consider where shelves will go in your home. Regardless of type, they will need to be positioned where their load can be supported properly. Bookshelves that must accommodate heavy loads should be positioned along a load-bearing wall, which can share some of the weight of the unit with the floor. Freestanding shelves more than 4 feet (122 cm) high should be outfitted with anti-topple devices and checked for stability.

> **How Much Shelving Do You Need?** To do this, lay out all the items you want to put on the shelves on the floor and measure their length. If you want to display collectibles on shelves, such as pots, remember to add extra inches to this figure. Always overestimate how much linear space you will need, especially if you're still collecting or amassing the objects or items that will fill the shelves.

> **How Sturdy Do They Need to Be?** The shorter and thicker the shelves, the sturdier they will be, and the heavier the load, the shorter the span of a shelf should be. Three-quarter inch (1.9 cm) shelves should not be longer than 24 inches (61 cm); 1-inch (2.5 cm) shelves can be 32 inches (81.3 cm) long. Shelves can exceed 32 inches (81.3 cm) in length, but keep in mind that these will need additional support and sturdy fabricating materials.

> **Do You Want Ready-Made or Custom-Built Shelves?** Ready-made shelves range from cheap knock-offs to exquisite cases that are considered fine furniture. Fiberboard and particleboard covered with laminate or veneers are used for inexpensive pieces, while veneered plywood or solid wood are used for higher-quality shelves. In either case, the benefits of ready-made units are obvious because they are ready to use immediately and are portable when you move. Because of the cost and time involved, custom-built shelves are generally made of finer materials. Costs vary depending on the size and scope of the job and materials chosen.

ATTICS, BASEMENTS, AND GARAGES Basements and attics can add significant living and storage space to a home, and often these areas combine both functions. A home office or playroom in an attic, or craft corners and hobby centers in basements, require room for activities and storage. And often, the structural features of the space can be used to create storage, or the storage components used in the space can define its activity centers. For instance, the space between the rafters in an attic can be converted to makeshift closets or shelves, or shelves can be hung from the collar beams or nailed between the exposed studs, while the entire windowless perimeter of a basement is ideal for banks of shelves. Or, shelves can become a freestanding wall to separate areas that coexist in the same basement or attic, such as the office and playroom. Both of these levels also offer ideal spots for inactive storage, and again, thoughtful design can allow them to accommodate this function with other uses.

Garages can become perfect areas for seasonal storage or craft centers, especially if a home is short on space. However, they are also the spot where many other items used in maintaining a home must be stored, such as lawn mowers, snow blowers, gardening supplies, power and hand tools, garbage bins, and more. Sporting equipment such as bicycles, wagons, fishing and camping gear, roller blades, skateboards, and balls are also stashed here, along with cars—which are ostensibly the primary purpose for even having a garage. Like other areas in a home, they can and should be outfitted with attractive and carefully planned built-in or

__right top__
Create an activity center or home office in a corner of the basement or garage with the right kind of storage. It doesn't call for anything fancy; shelves fitted with boxes can hold everything from tools and craft materials to old records and files.

__right bottom__
Outfit under cabinet areas in basements or garages with Peg-Board for versatile storage.

freestanding storage. For instance, most of the items stashed in garages can be put on heavy-duty hooks attached to the walls to free up valuable floor space for vehicles. And it pays to have a set of heavy-duty shelves on hand to store heavy items, such as cans of paint or bulk cleaning supplies.

Reserve these spaces for items of value you will really use or want to keep for posterity, not junk. Items stashed in inactive storage tend to stay there and escape scrutiny, so things that no longer have any personal meaning tend to linger instead of getting cleaned out. Also, make sure you pack items away so they'll withstand the tests of time, be it water seepage, humidity, or the appetites of various critters.

above top
Put aside the notion of a messy, grimy garage and get organized with store-bought cabinets that emulate the look of built-ins. The best part of this equation is that items stay clean and out of the way of larger items that must be stored in the space, such as bicycles and a lawn mower.

above bottom
Store-bought components can be used to turn a low, narrow space under the eaves into a spacious closet. Mining these spaces can add significant storage and living space to a home.

> **Quick Custom** Storage and Shelving

Interesting shelving systems are easier to put together than you might expect. Consider the following do-it-yourself ideas, which require little effort yet offer substantial rewards.

> **Corner Shelves** Claim the space in a corner with triangularly shaped shelves. The simplest way to do this is to cut shelves, or have them cut, to the desired size. (A shelf with 12-inch [30cm] -long sides will have a 17-inch [43 cm] -long angled edge.) Next, fasten strips of narrow molding to the walls with finishing nails on each side, stopping 1 inch [2.5 cm] shy of the actual corner. (For shelves with 12-inch [30 cm] -long sides, 10 inches [25 cm] is ideal). Because of the configuration of the corner, no other form of support is necessary. Corner shelves can be easily turned into a mock cupboard by surrounding them with molding, adding a cross piece right below a shelf about halfway down the stack

and at the floor, and cutting a panel door to fit between the two cross pieces and cover the bottom shelves. Attach the door with hinges, and paint the cupboard with a decorative pattern or faux finish.

> **Quick Stacks** Sturdy benches found in stores can be stacked on top of each other to create instant custom storage systems. Stack four benches at the foot of a bed (two on each side, two high) to create a footboard that can accommodate quilts or gym equipment, or stack six to ten benches (three to five on each side, three to five high) in a back hallway to hold hats, scarves and gloves, or briefcases and schoolbooks for family members. They

can also be fitted with decorative bins. File drawers can also be stacked, *tansu* style, to make an interesting arrangement and painted with decorative motifs.

> **Between the Studs** When storage space is at a premium, build your own shelving system in the recessed compartments between the studs. Studs are the vertical wooden supports, usually spaced 16 inches (40 cm) apart, that are used to frame and support a structure and are covered with plaster or drywall in each room in a home. Cut out the drywall or plaster between the studs, build shelves to fit the space, and finish them with paint. Use molding around the edges for a polished, built-in appearance.

above
Stack metal file drawers and cabinets *tansu*-style to create a visually arresting and functional storage system.

<u>**above**</u>
Build your own shelves in the recessed compartments
between the studs in your walls. By using luxuriously
thick slabs of wood and just the right lighting, they
can look quite professional.

> **Organizing** Your Stuff

Clever storage solutions and ideas
for the way you really live

top left

Wheels enhance the utility of a sturdy canvas hamper. Traditionally employed in laundries, this type of storage is ideal for artists, writers, and anyone who works with a lot of bits and pieces. Items can be sorted easily, and stacked-up goods can be rolled out of sight.

top right

For a clean, modern way to keep a bathroom organized, try a hanging metal rack for towels, blankets, or other linens.

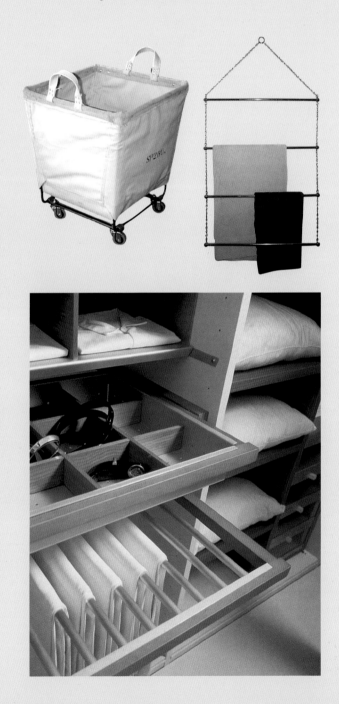

right

Rollout shelves are ideal for getting to stored accessories and clothing—and for helping to keep closets tidy. Especially handy in spots where the closet or shelf is deep or very low to the floor.

Don't let an odd-shaped area go to waste. This metal storage system has what it takes to wrap around corners and maximize space, making use of every available inch.

Make Your Own Storage

Though there are scores of storage products on the market to choose from for use in your home, you don't always have to go shopping to find a solution to your needs. Or perhaps you may long for something a bit more singular or personalized than the stock canisters, boxes, baskets, and bins sold at the local mass merchant or container store.

With a bit of creativity and elbow grease, it is possible to devise your own storage options. In fact, you usually have some of the materials you need at home if you look hard enough. For instance, instead of buying special cardboard boxes for photos, refurbish old shoeboxes with contact paper and put them to work. Or recycle pretty vintage suitcases as storage for out-of-season clothes, stacking them in a room to form a side table.

But best of all, the storage options you develop on your own can fulfill your needs for utility and wants for a specific decorative aesthetic. How? Here are a few ideas on how to create storage options in your home that blend substance and style.

Do you have a large collection of postcards that you just don't want to throw away? Here's an inventive way to keep them neat and tidy. All of the boards are cut out in advance, then glued to a single piece of cloth. There is also a wonderful economy of time and materials. Many of the boards share the same dimensions and are cut with a minimum of measuring. And the scrap fabric is recycled in the finishing. This box will hold a 2" (5 cm) stack of postcards.

Postcard Box

Materials

- Binder's board, 60 point
- Bookcloth
- Decorative paper
- Elastic cord
- 1 button (or more, for decorating)
- 1 postcard or photograph
- Sewing thread
- PVA, mixture and paste
- Pressure-sensitive adhesive

GETTING STARTED GATHERING THE DECORATIONS

- Gather the contents of the box: postcards received from friends and family, postcards from your travels, or handmade postcards.
- Collect buttons: One will serve as the clasp, so make sure it is sturdy. The others will be for decoration.
- Decide on decorative paper to line the inside of the box.

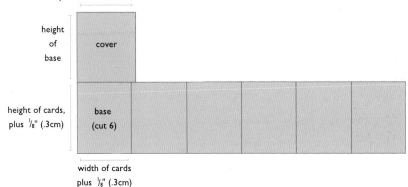

width of base,
plus one board thickness

height of base — cover

height of cards, plus 1/8" (.3cm) — base (cut 6)

width of cards plus 1/8" (.3cm)

1 Cut out all of the boards, following the layout above. Cut 6 pieces to:

Height = height of postcards plus 1/8" (.3 cm)
Width = width of postcards plus 1/8" (.3 cm)

REMEMBER: Grain must run from head to tail. Label one piece "base," and set it aside. Label one piece "fore-edge flap," and set it aside. Cut one piece in half, crosswise; trim a sliver off each piece, crosswise. Label these boards "head flap" and "tail flap," and set them aside.

Cut two 2" (5 cm) deep strips off one of the remaining boards, crosswise. Label these boards "head wall" and "tail wall." Cut a lengthwise strip, 2" (5 cm) plus one board thickness in width, from one of the remaining boards. Label it "fore-edge wall." From the last remaining board cut a lengthwise strip that measures 2" (5 cm) plus two board thicknesses in width. Label it "spine wall." If you wish to make a shallower or deeper box, adjust the depth of these walls accordingly. You have now used up all six pieces. The final board, the cover board, is cut separately. Cut a board to:

Height = height of base board

Width = width of base board plus one board thickness

Label this piece "cover." From a leftover board, cut a narrow strip a scant two board-thicknesses in width (grain long for ease in cutting). This will be your joint spacer. You need only one spacer; it will be reused several times.

2 Cut a piece of bookcloth large enough to accommodate all of the boards with a generous margin. This box requires a piece of cloth approximately 22" (56 cm) square. Trim off the selvage, or bound edge, of the cloth. Do not trim any other cloth until the boards have been glued into place.

Glue the boards onto the cloth. Place the cloth, wrong side up, on newsprint. Arrange the boards on the cloth, making sure the grain direction of the cloth and the board is the same. On a separate stack of newsprint, glue the boards one at a time and press them onto the cloth. The same spacer will be used between all of the boards (see drawing below). Start with the cover board and work your way across the horizontal plane before gluing the vertical elements. When all of the boards are in place, turn the cloth over and rub down with your folder to make sure no air bubbles remain.

Trim the turn-in margins. Cut a scrap board to approximately 3/4" (2 cm). Use it to trace around the edges of the boards, drawing the turn-in allowance. Slide a cutting mat under the cloth and trim, using a knife and straight-edge.

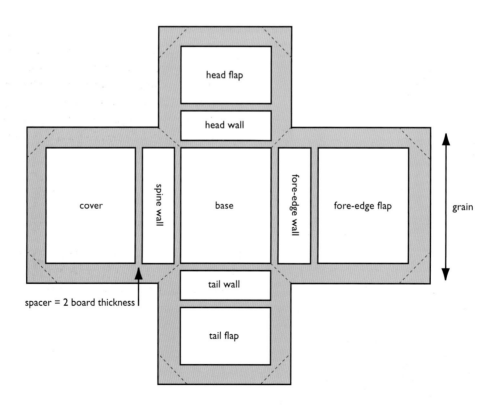

3 Cut the cloth at the four corners of the base board, slicing diagonally through the turn-in, cutting in as close as possible to the tip of the board. Cut off the (8) triangles at the outer corners of the boards. Stay 1 1/2 board thicknesses away from the tip of the boards.

4 Glue the turn-ins. Start with the eight turn-ins that touch the walls; finish with the four turn-ins that land on the flaps. Use your 1/2" (1 cm) brush. Before gluing, slip narrow strips of newsprint under each turn-in. Glue. Remove the waste strip and press the cloth against the board edge. With the edge of your bone folder, work the cloth into the two joints, pressing back and forth until the fabric has stuck. With the broad side of your bone folder, press the cloth onto the boards. Work through a waste sheet to prevent marking the cloth.

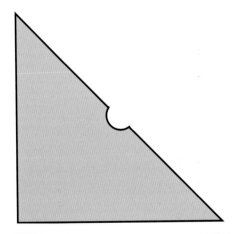

5 Cover the tips of the base board. Cut four triangles from the fabric off-cuts and trim them to fit the corners of the base board. They should match up with, and complete, the edges of the turn-ins. Do not overlap the fabric. If necessary, scoop out a slight crescent shape along the long side of the triangle to keep the right angle formed by the vertical and horizontal planes clean and crisp.

6 Glue out one triangle. Press it lightly onto the base board. Immediately work the fabric into the two joints, pressing back and forth with your bone folder.

7 Mold the cloth around the tip of the board, patting down any loose threads. Repeat with the other three triangles.

8 Decorate the box. Design the cover. Include in your design one button that will be the box's closure. If affixing a photograph or a postcard, use a pressure-sensitive adhesive to adhere the artwork to the cover; eventually, the card will be sewn into place. Arrange the button(s) on the cover. Punch holes through the boards to correspond with the button holes. Sew on the button(s).

9 Note: If not incorporating buttons into your design, punch holes through the card in strategic places—the corners, for example—and stitch the card in place. The pressure-sensitive adhesive is not secure enough for permanent attachment. Punch two holes in the fore-edge wall for the elastic cord. Thread both ends of the cord through the holes; adjust cord for the proper tension. If desired, thread a button or two onto the cord, to disguise these holes. Cut two shallow channels in the board and tip down the ends of the cord using undiluted PVA. Be persistent: The elastic does not want to stick! Press with your folder to flatten the cord. One or two careful hits with a hammer sometimes does the trick.

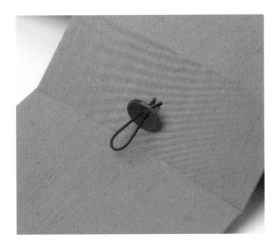

10 Cover the inside walls. Cut four strips of cloth from your leftovers. These strips will extend from the base board to the flaps, covering the walls. They are cut to fit approximately one board thickness away from the outer edges of the box. Cut two strips for the spine and fore-edge walls:

Height = height of walls minus two board thicknesses
Width = depth of walls plus 2" (5 cm)
Cut two strips for the head and tail walls:
Height = depth of wall plus 2" (5 cm)
Width = width of walls minus two board thicknesses

11 Grain should run from head to tail. Glue out the spine wall covering. Position the cloth on the base board, even with the turn-ins and centered heightwise. With the edge of your bone folder, quickly press the cloth into the joint nearest the base; smooth the cloth across the spine wall; press it into the second joint; smooth the cloth onto the cover board. Repeat with the other three wall coverings.

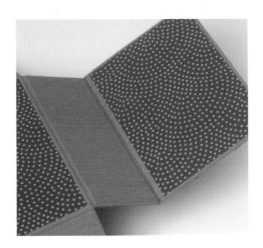

12 Line the box. Cut five pieces of paper to line all panels of the box. These papers are cut to fit approximately one board thickness away from all four edges of each panel.

This practical and pretty display provides handy storage for CDs, photos, or letters. Perfect for wedding or baby shower gifts, the boxes can be customized to any décor. This project uses plain or patterned grosgrain ribbon as a textural accent, as well as copper metallic rubbing compound for a distressed paint finish on the lid edges. Handwrite special words or phrases on the boxes to further personalize the set, and top it all off with a painted wooden medallion and bead.

Decorated Papier-Mâché Boxes

Materials
- three papier-mâché boxes
- wood medallion and round
- wooden bead
- craft acrylic paint in cream, mint, light sage, and metallic copper
- thick white glue
- 3 yards (2.7 m) of 1" (2 cm) grosgrain ribbon
- copper metallic rubbing compound
- gold metallic paint marker
- matte acrylic spray sealer (optional)
- general craft supplies

VARIATION Glue dried flower petals to the box sides and store seeds or other garden supplies.

TIP Practice handwriting the words on a scrap piece of cardboard before writing on the box.

MAKES THREE BOXES

1 Paint boxes and lids in desired base color of acrylic paint with a foam brush. Let dry. Paint the wood medallion and bead with the metallic copper acrylic paint and let dry.

2 Paint freehand designs on the sides of boxes using cream-colored acrylic paint with a round paintbrush, using "comma" brush strokes for swirls and the brush end to make dots. Let dry.

3 Apply ribbon accents to the boxes using small amounts of thick white glue.

4 With your fingertips, apply copper metallic rubbing compound to the edges of the lids. Handwrite desired words on the edges with a metallic paint marker.

5 Glue the medallion and bead to the top of the small box. Seal entire project with matte acrylic spray sealer if desired.

Here's a whimsical decorative box that's useful for storing keys, jewelry, or small treasures. This easy decoupage technique uses white craft glue and water-based varnish to seal the images. Decorate the container with a collage of themed images and cutout text, or try an eclectic mix of similar hues. Begin with an unfinished box and paint or stain it to coordinate with your chosen images, or revitalize and recycle an old box. Line the box with colorful fibrous paper to protect and finish the inside.

Keepsake Box

Materials
- wooden box
- printed images
- decorative paper
- white craft glue
- bone folder (optional)
- water-based satin varnish
- general craft supplies

VARIATION Liven up other pieces of wooden furniture, such as chair backs, CD cabinets, and coffee tables with decoupaged images.

TIP To smooth air bubbles and remove excess glue from placed prints easily, place a sheet of wax paper over the image and rub gently with a bone folder.

MAKES ONE BOX

1 Sand wooden box lightly with fine sandpaper. Wipe away dust with a slightly misted paper towel.

2 Cut images from old books, magazines, or color-copied reproductions with small, sharp scissors or a craft knife and cutting mat. Trim decorative paper to desired size. Spread white craft glue onto the back of each cutout image and paper with a foam brush and apply to desired area of the box. Rub images with a soft, dry cloth to press out any air bubbles or excess glue. Remove any excess glue with a slightly damp sponge. Allow to dry.

3 Apply six coats of water-based satin varnish with a foam brush, brushing each coat in alternating directions, allowing to dry thoroughly between coats. When final coat of varnish has completely dried, lightly rub the box with fine steel wool.

1.

2.

3.

Variation

It may be a gift to be simple, but it isn't always easy—a single lower-case letter against a solid background leaves no place to hide mistakes! These classic Shaker boxes are painted with milk paint, a dead-flat finishing paint made from one of the oldest paint recipes known. Choose "c" for cosmetics, "s" for safety pins, or pick a letter simply because it's beautiful.

Shaker Boxes

Materials

- unfinished wooden Shaker boxes
- milk paint in two colors
- transfer paper
- pen
- foam brushes
- disposable container for mixing paint
- medium-sized sable flat brush
- small round sable brush
- fine sandpaper
- sealer

VARIATION Using two tints of wood stain also works well on Shaker boxes. Because stain is so fluid, create a boundary between the letter and the background by etching a border line on the wooden lid around the letter with a craft knife for sharp definition between stained areas. Alternatively, try painting masking fluid (an easily removed liquid mask) around the letterform for a softer border between stain tints.

---

1. Following manufacturer's directions for mixing and applying milk paint, paint the boxes with a base coat of paint and a foam brush. In the example, one coat of the darker shade of paint was enough, but the lighter paint needed two coats for even coverage. Let dry completely. Enlarge your chosen letter to the correct size to fit on the box's lid. Transfer the letter to the lid with either white or graphite transfer paper, depending on the darkness of your chosen background. Try to keep the transfer lines just within the letter's border so the lines will not show on the finished box.

2. Mix the milk paint for the letterform. Using a sable flat brush, begin filling in the letterform. Avoid loading the brush with too much paint. Turn the box and the brush edge to create a sharp border for the letter. Fill in corner details with a small round brush. Continue applying a light coat of paint until the letter is filled. The paint will dry unevenly at first, so don't worry if coverage is not perfect on the first coat. Be careful not to rest your hand on the working surface while painting.

3. When the first coat is complete, let dry completely. Lightly sand any bubbles in the paint. Add a second light coat of paint to the letter, let dry, and, if necessary, add a third. Be careful to keep coats light and to let them dry well between applications, or cracks may appear (though cracks can look good, too!). When the lettering is complete and dry, sand the box with fine sandpaper to add distressed edges and to even any dried paint bubbles. Finish with a sealer such as Danish oil.

These handwoven baskets are actually recycled grocery bags. The printing from the bags lends an old-time graphic appeal to the final project. Paper grocery bags are surprisingly strong—the finished baskets are quite durable. This easy weaving technique can be adapted to create baskets of many sizes and shapes. Use them to hold paper clips and pens at your desk, or create a series of baskets in varying sizes for an eclectic display. Refer to diagrams A-D while making this project.

Woven Brown Bag Basket

VARIATION Use decorative paper to create small baskets for party favors and candy.

TIP Work with even numbers of strips and plan basket size in advance. The larger the basket, the wider, longer, and stronger the strips should be.

MAKES ONE BASKET

1 Cut off the bottom of one grocery bag at the folding line and discard the bottom section. Fold the top section in half, open end to open end; cut into two pieces along fold. Cut pieces open along seam line to create two strips that are approximately 6" x 36" (15 cm x 91 cm). Fold each strip in half lengthwise, then fold each long side in toward the center again, creating long strips of four layers. Repeat for remaining grocery bags.

2 Trim six paper strips to 28" (71 cm) lengths and place side by side. Weave four of the remaining 36" (91 cm) strips into the six shorter strips in an over-and-under pattern, leaving at least 6" (15 cm) edges on all sides (see diagram A). Fold up edge strips perpendicular to the woven base, and clip vertically in pairs with clothespins (see diagram B).

3 Beginning in the middle of one side, weave one paper strip around perimeter using an over-and-under pattern (see diagram C). Repeat for two more strips, starting each row on a different side of the basket. Tighten the basket until no open spaces are visible between strips. Glue strip ends in place. Crease the corners and edges. Trim the top edge evenly. Put a drop of glue on the top horizontal strip at each vertical strip and clip with clothespins. Allow to dry; remove clothespins.

4 Fold the remaining paper strip over the top edge of the basket to finish (see diagram D). Clip in place with clothespins and crease corners. Blanket-stitch twine around the top strip to secure in place, sewing between intersection of the weave.

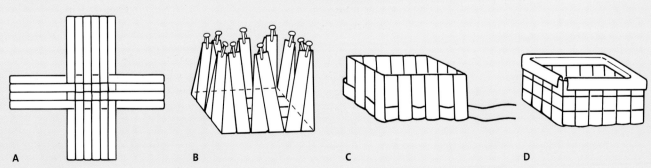

A   B   C   D

KEYS

4

1

5

2

6

3

1.

2.

3.

Some of the best ideas come from unusual places. What better approach to storage problems than to use those shoeboxes lurking in the closet. Shoeboxes are the perfect size and shape for millions of things. This simple project wraps them in plain white paper so the boxes' original printing doesn't show through. To really conquer clutter, divide the interior into individual compartments. This makes finding even the smallest object easy and quick.

Elegant Shoebox Storage

Materials

- 5 to 7 empty shoeboxes
- heavyweight white butcher paper, mailing paper, or decorative wrapping paper
- aerosol adhesive
- transparent tape
- corrugated cardboard
- a razor knife or scissors
- steel ruler
- marker pen
- numeral stencil
- white glue (optional)

1 Start with the lid and cut out a rectangle of paper large enough to fold over the lip of the box lid on all sides. Attach with spray adhesive, or simply fix with tape. Aim for a tight, smooth finish, so the paper will not tear in daily use. Wrap the box next, taking care to leave a 3" (8 cm) length of paper to fold over the box lip on all four sides. Shorter lengths may look sloppy when the box is open—they also may not adhere as well. When you've wrapped several boxes and their lids, use the marking pen to label each box with a large numeral or name—something that will stand out and help you find the contents easily.

2 Internal dividers for small containers aren't always easy to find: for ready-made stock, try housewares shops (they often have them leftover from packing materials). To make your own, measure the internal length and width of the box, then cut two pieces of corrugated cardboard to fit the length measurement, three or four pieces for the width. Divide and mark the two long strips in three. Use the ruler as a cutting guide (to make straight cuts) and cut thick slots half-way through each strip (as shown), to create an interlocking grid.

3 Size the grid to match whatever it is the boxes will hold. You may want to use a bit of white glue or tape to reinforce the grid once it is assembled, to make it more durable. You can paint or decorate the grids to add to their appeal.

No glue, paste, or complicated cuts, this box is simply two pieces of paper joined at the base with strips of pressure-sensitive adhesive. Since it is such an austere construction, the Stationery Box needs a paper with character and body to give it charm. If the color is vibrant, it needs very little ornamentation: a button or two and a piece of bright thread are enough. The paper used here is a lustrous handmade. Its linen content gives the paper both strength and tactility.

Stationery Box

Materials
- A good-quality handmade paper
- Thread
- Buttons
- Elastic cord
- Pressure-sensitive adhesive on a roll
- PVA

NOTE: Steps 2 through 8 and step 10 are illustrated with scale models of the actual box.

GETTING STARTED CUTTING THE FIRST PIECE OF PAPER
- Cut out the first piece to the following dimensions:
  Height = height of object to be boxed (referred to as "object" hereafter)
  Width = width of object, plus twice the thickness of the object, plus 2"- 4" (5 -10 cm), depending on the size of the box.
- If you intend to sew through the spine and fore-edge walls (as in the box pictured), increase this width measurement by approximately 1/4" (.5 cm) since the stitching on the inside of the box juts into the base, diminishing its overall width.

1.

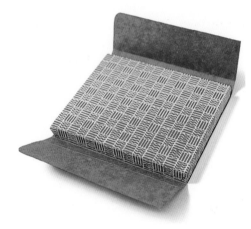

2.

1 Score the paper by centering the object on the paper and making two pinpricks, to the left and right of the object, on the tail edge of the paper. Score and sharply crease the paper.

2 Form the spine and fore-edge walls. Measure the thickness of the object and transfer this measurement to your paper, with pinprick markings, to the outside of the previously scored lines. (To measure for thickness, measure the depth of the object to be boxed. For example, from the top card to the bottom card in a deck of cards.) Score and sharply crease the paper. Round the sharp corners, at head only.

3 Cut out the second piece: Height = three times the height of the object plus twice its thickness. Width = width of object enclosed in the first piece. Grain must run from spine to fore-edge.

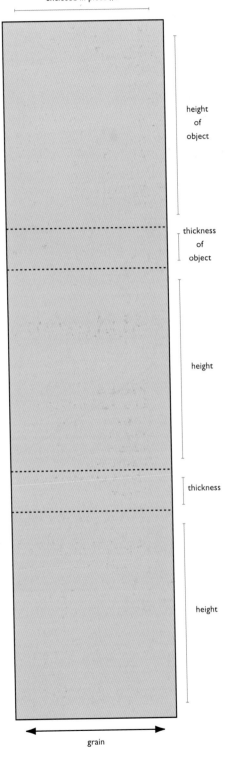

width of object, enclosed in piece #1

height of object

thickness of object

height

thickness

height

grain

3.

4.

5.

4 Score the paper by centering the (enclosed) object on the paper and making two pinpricks, to the top and bottom of the object, on the spine edge of the paper. Score and sharply crease the paper.

Form the head and tail walls. Measure the thickness of the object to be enclosed and transfer this measurement to your paper, with pinprick markings to the outside of the previously scored lines. Score and sharply crease the paper.

5 Trim head and tail flaps to desired shape and depth. Round off all sharp edges on head flap.

6a.

6b.

6a Sew on button and apply reinforcement patches. Decide on the placement of the buttons and elastic cord on the head and tail flaps. Punch holes.

6b Before sewing, cut and glue small patches of paper over punched area, either inside or out. Insert cord and sew on buttons.

7a.

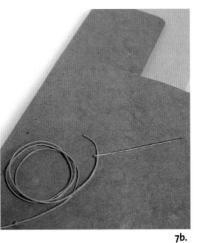

7b.

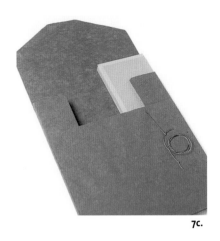

7c.

7a, b, c If sewing the spine and fore-edge walls, punch holes through the tail flap, the flanges under the flap, and through corresponding areas on the spine and fore-edge walls. Do not sew.

8.

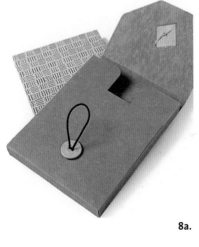

8a.

8 Attach the two units by applying strips of pressure-sensitive adhesive to the second piece, in the areas illustrated.

8a Peel off backing paper on the base area only, and stick the two units together. If omitting decorative stitching, peel off backing paper on the tail flap and carefully align this flap with the spine and fore-edge flanges; press down into place. If sewing, thread two needles. Start on the inside of the tail flap, and sew toward the head in an overcast stitch, sewing up both sides simultaneously. When the sewing is complete, sneak inside and peel off backing paper on tail flap; press the flap onto the flange.

1.   TEA

2.   TEA

3.   TEA

A set of ceramic canisters is made modern with the addition of deep painted shadows that merely hint at the letterform creating them. A simple and bold color scheme and wide letter spacing add to the strong graphic effect. Sharp edges and smooth paint coverage are the keys to this decorative technique, so a mask is made from self-adhesive vinyl paper before applying the paint. Try this lettering style on glass or ceramic vases, kitchen cabinet doors, or any project that would be enhanced by a modern-styled label.

Kitchen Canisters

Materials
- ceramic canister set
- lettering reference guide (computer generated)
- solvent-based air-drying paint for ceramics (Pebeo Ceramique works well)
- vinyl self-stick shelf lining paper or airbrush masking film
- disposable medium-pointed brush, or medium-pointed brush and turpentine brush cleaner
- tracing paper
- transfer paper
- pen
- craft knife

VARIATION Because the unpainted area of the canister is masked, many decorative painting techniques can be utilized on the letters. Try spotting a contrasting shade of paint over the first shade by loading a stiff paintbrush or old toothbrush with paint and flicking the bristles with a gloved finger. Or, try sponging a complementary color over the base coat.

1. Enlarge the lettering guide to your chosen size. Draw a baseline on tracing paper. Trace the letters onto tracing paper and fill them in. Use a wide letter spacing, both to create a modern look and to allow space for a large shadow. These letters are the white space of the final letterforms—they provide a boundary only and won't be painted.

2. Place the tracing paper over the lettering guide again, but so that the next set you trace is evenly shifted down and to the right. Trace the letters and fill them in; this step is represented in black in this example. Draw connecting lines (dashed blue lines) between the original letters and the second set of letters at corresponding outside points. Not all points will need to be connected—with experience, you'll develop a feel for which ones are necessary.

3. Fill in the areas defined by the second set of letters and the interior of the connecting lines up to the border of the original letters. This will result in a deep shadow that, when the original set of letters is deleted, becomes the shadowed design. Transfer these shadow forms with transfer paper onto vinyl self-stick shelf lining paper that has already been smoothly applied to the ceramic canister. Cut out the shadow areas from the vinyl with a craft knife, using clean, sharp lines. Apply the paint according to manufacturer's directions; when paint has partially set, remove the vinyl paper quickly and smoothly. Small mistakes can be corrected with solvent and a cotton swab when wet, or by carefully scraping them off with a razor blade when dry.

Use paper to cover a simple wooden display case and turn it into a cozy rack for spices. This cabinet features origami papers for the background and uses a medium-weight highly textured paper to cover the exterior and the shelves. Although all the colors are different, they are all from a warm palette so they work together nicely and go with the warm-toned spices that they house. To secure the contents of each shelf, braid waxed cotton cord and string it across each opening.

Spice Case

Materials

- wooden display case with shelves
- coordinating medium-weight textured paper in three colors
- 4 sheets of coordinating origami paper
- collage glue
- small sponge brush
- scissors
- metal ruler
- pencil
- waxed cotton cord
- hammer
- 4 small nails

1 Measure, mark, and tear the papers for each section of the box according to the measurements of your wooden case. Use a different color for the inside dividers, the inside rim, and the outside rim. Tear, rather than cut, the paper along the lines. Firmly hold a metal ruler along one of your marks, then pull the paper up and towards you. This will give your papers a softer edge, which is more easily blended along a seam.

1.

2.

2 Measure, mark, and cut the sheets of origami paper for the back wall. Use a small sponge brush and collage glue to adhere the papers to the case. Smooth the papers from the center out to press out any air bubbles.

3.

3 To glue a sheet of paper, use a sponge brush to apply a thin layer of collage glue on the back of the paper and then place the paper in the appropriate area. Use a toothpick to position the paper evenly into the corners and along the straight edges of the wood. Use bits of torn paper to patch up any bare spots. Paper the inside dividers first; then cover the inside area of the rim. Finish by covering the outside rim of the case.

4.

4 Cut three lengths of waxed cotton cord that are three times the width of your shelf. Make an overhand knot in one end, then braid the three strands to the desired length. Tie another overhand knot to secure the braid. Cut off any excess cord 1" (3 cm) from the knot on each end. Repeat to make a braid for each shelf. Lay one braid across the case approximately 1" (3 cm) above the shelf. Gently hammer a small nail into each knot, centering the nail in the edge of the wood. Repeat to attach each braided cord. Now your shelf is ready to hang and fill with spice jars.

TIP Apply a thin layer of acrylic varnish or decoupage medium over the paper, if desired. This will create a more translucent effect and give the paper a sheen while also protecting it. A varnish will likely darken the color of your paper, so keep this in mind when you are choosing your colors. If you don't choose to put a finish coat on the paper, it will retain its matte appearance.

VARIATION Here, the case is used as a memory holder. Rather than using origami papers for the background, it was covered with the same paper used on the sides. We chose a cool palette, and then tore and inset coordinating squares of paper over each background area. White paper roses and buds were attached with hot glue, but instead of displaying flowers, you can chose to feature other personal mementos such as seashells, seedpods, or memorabilia from your travels.

Its charm is in its size (2 1/2" [6 cm] square), as well as in its materials. The Jewelry Box consists of two units: a four-walled tray and a case. The case extends slightly beyond the edges of the tray, creating a small lip. Once assembled, the front of the case becomes the hinged lid of the box.

Keep in mind the rules of boxmaking: Wherever hinging occurs, use cloth instead of paper. The one exception is in the use of Momi papers. If not using these resilient Japanese papers, use bookcloth for the case construction. In the directions, the case material is referred to as cloth.

Jewelry Box

Materials
- Binder's board
- Museum board, two ply (liners)
- Cloth or paper (tray)
- Cloth or Momi paper (case)
- Bone clasp
- Ribbon
- PVA, mixture and paste

GETTING STARTED CUTTING THE BOARDS
- Cut out the boards for the tray following the layout shown.
- Pay attention to the logic of the cuts, which ensures that all parts sharing the same measurements are cut in sequence, and with a minimum of marking.
- Base:
  > Height = desired height of tray, plus two covering thicknesses
  > Width = desired width of tray, plus two covering thicknesses
- Head and tail walls:
  > Height = desired depth of tray, plus one board thickness
  > Width = desired width of tray, plus two covering thicknesses
- Spine and fore-edge walls:
  > Height = height of base board, plus two board thicknesses
  > Width = desired depth of tray, plus one board thickness

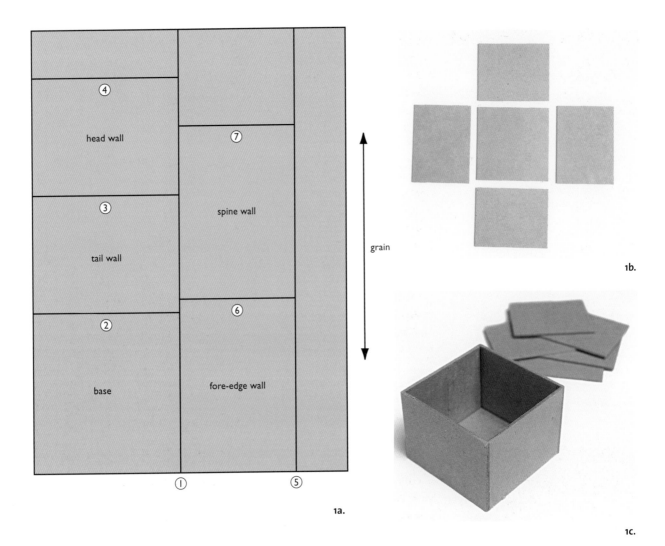

head wall

④

③

tail wall

②

base

⑦

spine wall

⑥

fore-edge wall

①　⑤

grain

1a.

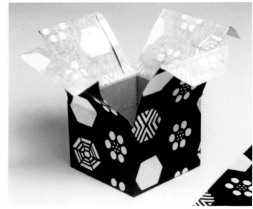

1b.

1c.

1a-c Construct the tray using full-strength PVA, paint a thin line of glue along the edge of the head wall where it touches the base. Wipe away excess glue, making sure to maintain right angle of head wall and base. Glue the tail wall by gluing along the edge touching the base and edge that meets the fore-edge wall. Glue spine wall by gluing along the edge touching the base and the two edges that meet the head and tail walls. Let the tray set until dry (15 minutes) and sand any rough joints.

2a Cover the tray. Cut out the covering material, a strip twice the depth of the tray plus 1 1/2" (4 cm), long enough to wrap around all four walls plus 1/2" (1 cm), and width should be twice the depth plus 1 1/2". If your decorative paper is not long enough, piece together two shorter strips, making sure that the seam falls on a corner of the tray.

2a.

2b.

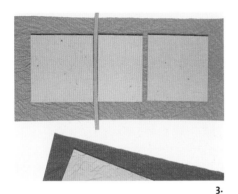

3.

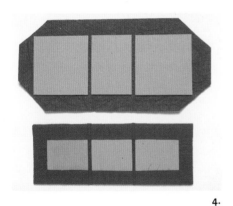

4.

5.

2b Cover the tray by pasting the backside of your paper. Position tray, with the bottom facing you, approximately 3/4" (2 cm) away from the long edge of the paper and 1/2" (1 cm) away from the short edge. Crease the 1/2" (1 cm) extension around the corner and onto the wall. Roll the tray, making sure to form snug right angle at the corners. Finish by pasting edges inside box. Trim any excess.

3 Cut out the three case boards to the following dimensions. Remember that the grain must run from head to tail on all boards.

Front and Back:

Height = height of tray, plus two board thicknesses

Width = width of tray, plus one board thickness

Spine:

Height = height of tray, plus two board thicknesses

Width = depth of tray (Here's an easy and accurate way to get this measurement: Sharply crease a small piece of scrap paper to form a right angle; place the tray on top of this paper and push the tray snugly into the right angle; make a second, parallel crease, over the top of the tray. The distance between these two crease marks is the exact depth of your tray.)

From your scrap board, cut a slender strip a scant two board thicknesses in width. This will be used as a spacer when gluing up the case.

Next cut out the case cloth or Momi paper:

Height = height of boards, plus 1 1/2" (4 cm)

Width = width of boards, laid out with joint spacer plus 1 1/2" (4 cm)

4 Construct the case. Glue out the front board and place it on the cloth, approximately 3/4" (2 cm) away from all three edges. Press into place. Position the spacer against the spine edge of the board, glue the spine piece, position the spine on the cloth, and push it firmly against the spacer. Remove the spacer and place it on the other side of the spine. Glue the back board, position it on the cloth pushed firmly against the spacer, and press into place.

5 Cut the corners and finish the edges. Cut the inner hinge cloth:

Height = height of the tray

Width = width of case spine, plus 2" (5 cm)

Grain, as always, runs from head to tail. Cut shallow triangular wedges off all four corners of this cloth.

6.

6 Glue out the hinge cloth, center it on the spine, press the cloth firmly into the joints of the case with your bone folder, then onto the front and back case boards. Rub down well.

7a Attach the clasp. Feed the ribbon through the slit in the bone clasp. Place the tray in the case, close it, and position the bone clasp on the front of the case, in its desired location. (If making more than one box, prepare patterns for the placement of the ribbons on both front and back.) Mark the front of the case with two pinpricks, one on each side of the clasp directly below its slit. Remove the tray and arrange the case right side up on a piece of scrap board. Select a chisel to match the width of your ribbon. Holding the chisel vertically make two parallel chisel cuts, starting at the pinpricks and chiseling downward.

7a.

7b Angle the ends of a short piece of ribbon and push the ribbon down through the cuts to form a receiving loop for the clasp. Slide the clasp into the loop. Pull the ribbon ends snugly on the inside of the case. Guide the main ribbon to the back of the case; mark for its insertion and make one vertical slit. Feed both ends of the ribbon into this slit, and make the ribbon taut. On the inside of the case, spread the ribbon ends in opposite directions. With your knife trace the outlines of the ribbons, cutting and peeling up a shallow layer of board. Glue the ribbons into these recesses using undiluted PVA. Bone down this area well to make it as smooth as possible.

Next attach the tray to the case. Spread undiluted PVA onto the bottom of the tray; wipe away excess glue. Place the tray on the back case board. The spine edge of the case should be flush with the spine edge of the tray. Center the tray by height. This placement allows a small lip around the head, fore-edge, and tail. Hold the tray in position for a few minutes, until the glue begins to set. (Take care to keep the tray centered—it's quite a slippery creature at first!) Invert the case, place a board and hefty weight on top, and press for at least a half hour.

Spread undiluted PVA onto the spine wall of the tray; wipe away excess glue. Roll the tray onto the case, spine walls touching; slide a board and a weight into the tray, and press until dry.

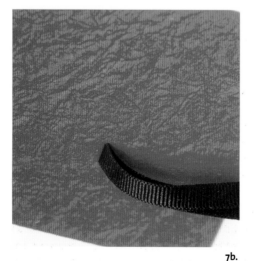

7b.

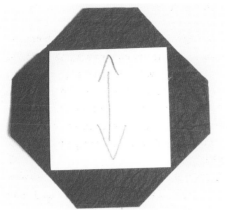

8a.

8 Line the box.

8a If lining with a medium or heavyweight paper, cut two pieces of paper to the same dimensions. (Remember to anticipate the stretch of the paper across the grain, and to cut it a bit narrower in width.)

Height = height of interior of tray, minus two paper thicknesses
Width = width of interior of tray, minus two paper thicknesses
Paste the papers and apply them to the bottom of the tray and the inside of the box lid. Press until dry.

8b If lining with a thin or fragile paper or with cloth, first "card" the material around lightweight boards, following the procedure below.

Cut out two pieces of museum board:
Height = height of interior of tray, minus 1/16" (0.15 cm)
Width = width of interior of tray, minus 1/16" (0.15 cm)

8b.

8c Cut out two pieces of covering paper:
Height = height of boards, plus 1 1/2" (4 cm)
Width = width of boards, plus 1 1/2" (4 cm)
Paste the papers, center the board on the papers, cut the corners and finish the edges.
Glue out one board with undiluted PVA and carefully lower it into the tray. Press until it takes hold. If your box is large, place newsprint, a board and a weight on top, and let sit for half an hour. Glue out the second board, and center it on the box lid. Press until it takes hold. Weight and let sit for one half hour to one hour.

8c.

It's easy to use a framework of cardboard covered with strips of paper to construct a small, mirrored cabinet. The craft of creating objects from layers of pasted paper has been around ever since waste paper has been available. This simple building technique allows a lot of flexibility in design—virtually any shape can be achieved, and the resulting sculptural pieces are lightweight and durable. Here, the base of the cabinet is cut from a flat sheet of cardboard that is folded up and around at the bottom to create the shelf. The shelf is then stabilized with the wrapped strips of paper. The mirror is taped to the back using a strong linen bookbinding tape.

Cosmetic Cabinet

Materials
- 1 sheet mat board
- newspapers torn into 1" (3 cm) strips
- white glue
- paintbrush
- paper tape
- acrylic paint
- craft knife
- metal ruler
- cutting mat
- linen bookbinding tape
- 4 1/2" x 4 1/2" (11 cm x 11 cm) beveled mirror
- acrylic varnish

VARIATION The paper strips and the finishes that are applied to them can create unique surface designs. Even just applying your strips in a specific direction can create a nice pattern. Here, the back plate of the cabinet was wrapped with all the strips moving outward from a diagonal center to look like rays of sun.

TIP Experiment with the texture and finish of your paper to make it resemble wood, stone, clay, or even metal. For example, you can add sand to your paint for a sandstone finish, paint a faux wood grain using feathers and umber washes, or add a thick layer of molding paste to give the impression of clay.

1 Photocopy template below at 160%. Trace the pattern for the cabinet onto the mat board. Using a craft knife, metal ruler, and cutting mat, cut out the pattern from the mat board. Score dashed lines. Turn the board over.

1.

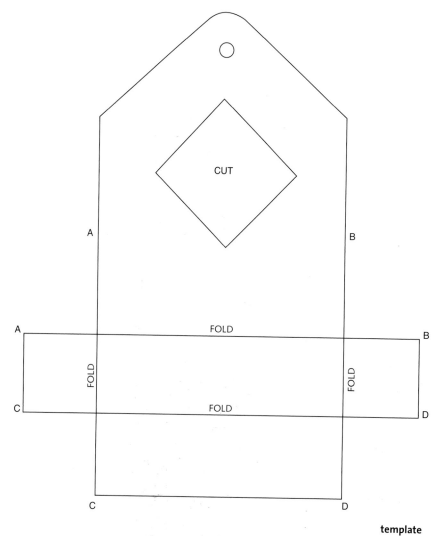

CUT

A

B

A   FOLD   B

FOLD   FOLD

C   FOLD   D

C   D

template

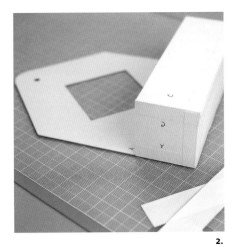

2.

2 Bend in point A to meet A, point B to meet B, and so forth, to make sure the edges of the shelf align. Adjust as needed. Secure the shelf edges with paper tape.

3 Tear newspapers into 1" (2.5 cm) strips. Pour white glue into disposable container and dilute by 10 percent. Using a paintbrush, apply the glue to a strip of newspaper and apply the strip to the cabinet; start by covering all adjoining edges, and apply the strips horizontally. Be sure to overlap edges of the strips as you go, and start and end the strips in a staggered fashion. Continue until the entire cabinet, front and back, has been covered with at least three layers of strips. Let dry completely for one to seven days, depending on the temperature.

3.

4.

4 Paint the entire cabinet with two coats of a solid color, allowing it to dry between coats. Then, using a barely damp sponge, gently give a rubbed coating of silver paint over the top, moving the sponge in the same direction as the strips of paper, leaving much of the base color still exposed. Let dry. Seal with two coats of acrylic varnish.

5 Place the mirror behind the opening and attach using linen bookbinding tape.

5.

> Resources

MAIL ORDER COMPANIES

Alsto's Handy Helpers
P.O. Box 1267
Galesburg, IL 61402
800-447-0048
www.alsto.com

Antique Hardware & Home Store
19 Buckingham Plantation Drive
Bluffton, SC 29910
800-422-9982

Home Decorators Collection
8920 Pershall Road
Hazelwood, MO 63042
800-245-2217
www.homedecorators.com

Renovator's Supply and Yield House
Renovator's Old Mill
Millers Falls, MA 01349
800-659-2211

The Museum of Useful Things
370 Broadway
Cambridge, MA 01239
617-576-3322
www.themut.com

NATIONAL RETAIL CHAINS

Bed, Bath & Beyond
650 Liberty Avenue
Union, NJ 07083
908-688-0888
www.bedbathandbeyond.com

California Closets
622 Lindaro Street
San Raphael, CA 94901
888-336-9709
www.californiaclosets.com

The Container Store
2000 Valwood Parkway
Dallas, TX 75234
800-733-3532
www.containerstore.com

Crate & Barrel
725 Landwehr Road
Northbrook, IL 60062
800-323-5461
888-249-4158
www.crateandbarrel.com

Ethan Allen
Ethan Allen Drive
P.O. Box 1966
Danbury, CT 06813
800-273-2191
www.ethanallen.com

Hold Everything
100 North Point Street
San Francisco, CA 94133
800-421-2264
www.holdeverything.com

Home Depot
2455 Paces Ferry Road
Atlanta, GA 30339
770-433-8211
www.homedepot.com

Ikea North America
496 W. Germantown Pike
Plymouth Meeting, PA 19462
800-434-4532
www.ikea.com

Luminaire
2331 Ponce de Leon Boulevard
Coral Gables, FL 33134
305-448-7367

Pier 1 Imports
P.O. Box 961020
Fort Worth, TX 76161
800-477-4371
www.pier1.com

Pottery Barn
Mail Order Department
P.O. Box 7044
San Francisco, CA 94120
800-922-5507
www.potterybarn.com

Restoration Hardware
104 Challenger Drive
Portland, TN 37148
800-762-1005
888-243-9720 for stores
www.restorationhardware.com

Williams-Sonoma
P.O. Box 7456
San Francisco, CA 94120
800-541-1262
www.williams-sonoma.com

INTERNATIONAL SOURCES

Isokon Plus
Turnham Green Terrace Mews
London W4 IQU
44-020-8994-0636 (phone)
44-020-8994-5635 (fax)
www.isokonplus.com

John Lewis
(stores nationwide)
Head Office
Oxford Street
London W1A 1EX, United Kingdom
tel. 020 7269 7711
www.johnlewis.co.uk

Selfridges
(stores London and Manchester)
Head Office
400 Oxford Street
London W1A 1AB, United Kingdom
tel. 020 629 1234
www.selfridges.co.uk

Heal's
(stores London, Kingston, Guildford)
Head Office
196 Tottenham Court Road
London W1T 7LQ, United Kingdom
tel: 020 7636 1666
www.heals.co.uk

HobbyCraft
(stores nationwide)
Head Office
Bournemouth, United Kingdom
tel. 01202 596100

> Credits

Fernando Bengoechea, 15; 40 (bottom); 47; 61; 142
Tony Berardi/Photofields/Powell-Kleinschmidt Design, 82
Tony Berardi/Photofields, 85
Antoine Bootz, 25; 38; 40 (top); 84
Andrew Bordwin, 70
Simon Brown/The Interior Archive, 50 (top)
Courtesy of California Closets, 29; 86; 87; 88; 89; 90; 91; 92; 96 (bottom); 97; 100 (bottom); 141 (left & middle)
Pieter Estersohn, 26; 51 (top)
Bill Geddes, 19
David Glomb, 83
John Hall, 37
Courtesy of Hold Everything, 5 (middle & second from bottom); 20, 21, 28 (bottom); 30 (top & middle); 54; 55 (top left & right); 58; 79 (bottom right); 95; 101; 140
Courtesy of Ikea, 52; 53; 55 (bottom); 67 (top); 68; 69; 76 (right); 77; 79 (left & top right); 141 (right)

Marco Lorenzetti/Hedrich Blessing, 32
Courtesy of Luminaire, 51 (bottom)
Richard Mandelkorn, 71
Peter Margonelli, 5 (second from top); 13; 17;
Nadia McKenzie/The Interior Archive, 59 (left)
Colin McRae/Kacy & Mark Marcinik, 44
Michael Moran, 9
Courtesy of The Museum of Useful Things, 28 (top); 30 (bottom); 31; 76 (top left); 78; 100 (top)
Michael Paul, 64; 65
Greg Premru, 22; 96 (top)
Ed Reeve, 5 (bottom); 50 (bottom)
Eric Roth, Design by Phinney 5 (top); 12 (top)
Eric Roth, 12 (bottom); 23 (top); 56
James Salomon, 80
Doug Snower/Leslie Jones Design, 73
Courtesy of Spiegel, 41; 45 (left)
Tim Street-Porter, 8; 11; 14; 94

John Sutton/Brayton & Hughes Design Studio, 42, 43
Brian Vanden Brink, 39
Fritz von der Schulenberg/The Interior Archive, 45 (right); 57; 59 (right); 63 (top); 99
Dominique Vorillon/Beate Works, 66; 93
William Waldron by Permission of House Beautiful, 35
Paul Warchol/LOT EK Architecture, 98
Paul Whicheloe, 4; 9
Elizabeth Whiting & Associates, 16; 63 (bottom); 67 (bottom)
Vincente Wolf, 23 (bottom); 27
Courtesy of Workbench, 74

Acknowledgments

This book would not be possible without the help of many individuals. First, my thanks to Martha Wetherill, acquisitions editor at Rockport, whose is always enthusiastic about anything involving design. Further thanks to my editors, Mary Ann Hall and Francine Hornberger. I am grateful for their persistence, diligence, and attention to detail, as well as their vigilant editing to make the text as specific and flawless as possible. Finally, in a visual book, superb graphic design is also critical; my thanks to Silke Braun and Leeann Leftwich, who made this book as stylish yet substantive as the subject matter. I would also like to thank the many photographers, interior designers, and architects whose work appear on these pages. Their efforts comprise the core of this book; without their creativity and vision this volume would not be possible.

About the Author

Lisa Skolnik is a regular contributor to the *Chicago Tribune* on design, entertaining, style, and family issues, and a city editor for *Metropolitan Home* magazine. Her work has also appeared in such publications as *Metropolitan Home* magazine, *Interiors* magazine, *Woman's Day*, *Good Housekeeping*, *Fodor's Chicago* guidebook and more. She is the author of fourteen books on design.

Skolnik lives and works in Chicago, where she has plenty of first-hand experience with storage issues thanks to the piles of possessions she has accrued with the help of her husband, Howard, and four children, Caroline, Sasha, Anastasia, and Theodora.